D1488829

Life
Begins
at Fifty

WALTER PITKIN, JR.

SIMON AND SCHUSTER

NEW YORK

SECOND PRINTING

The author wishes to thank the following publishers for permission to include
quotations from copyrighted materials:

DUELL, SLOAN & PEARCE: *Old Mr. Flood* by Joseph Mitchell, copyright 1943,
1944, 1945, 1948 by Joseph Mitchell. LITTLE, BROWN AND CO.: *Sixty-Five Plus* by
Clarence B. Randall, copyright © 1963 by Clarence Randall. G. & C. MERRIAM
Co.: Webster's Third New International Dictionary, copyright © 1961 by G. & C.
Merriam Co. THE NEW YORK TIMES: "Rodgers, at 60, Acts Younger than Spring-
time," copyright © 1962; the obituary of Victor Moore, copyright © 1962; "L. I.
Executive, 50, Joins Peace Corps to Work in Africa," copyright © 1964. All copy-
right by The New York Times Company. W. W. NORTON & CO. INC.: *Emotional
Problems of Living* by O. Spurgeon English and Gerald H. J. Pearson. SIMON AND
SCHUSTER, INC.: *Author! Author!* by P. G. Wodehouse, copyright © 1962 by P. G.
Wodehouse. THE UNIVERSITY OF CHICAGO PRESS: *The Meaning of Work and Re-
tirement* by Eugene A. Friedmann, Robert J. Havighurst, *et al.*, copyright 1954 by
The University of Chicago. THE VIKING PRESS: *The Letters of Sacco and Van-
zetti*, Marion Frankfurter, Ed., copyright © 1928, 1956 by The Viking Press, Inc.

LIBRARY OF CONGRESS CATALOG CARD NUMBER: 65-11978

MANUFACTURED IN THE UNITED STATES OF AMERICA

BY AMERICAN BOOK-STRATFORD PRESS, INC., NEW YORK

DESIGNED BY EVE METZ

AFFECTIONATELY DEDICATED TO ALL
THE 5,480 AMERICANS BORN JUST
FIFTY YEARS AGO TODAY—
HAPPY BIRTHDAY!

Contents

Do you take it I would astonish?
Does the daylight astonish? Does the early redstart
twittering through the woods?
Do I astonish more than they?

This hour I tell things in confidence,
I might not tell everybody, but I will tell you.
—WALT WHITMAN, "Song of Myself"

Foreword

DEAR READER, *what you hold in your hand is not a cure-all for the ills of life; as I write this, no panacea, whether in words or in pills, has yet proved out.*

Nor is it a reference book. Nor does it tell you whether the peonies grow redder in Florida or Arizona, or whether mutual funds are a better investment than a piece of downtown real estate in Allentown, Pennsylvania.

I think of it as a deference book—a book written out of deference to the intelligence and the hopes of those curious enough to read it for the light it may shed on the daily life and the future of today's fifty-year-old.

Most of the book is downright serious; I'm sure you will agree with that statement. Some of it, out of deference to a common human need for gaiety, is frivolous—maybe even funny. Perhaps, after reading it, you will agree with me that some of the frivolous parts are serious too—depending on how you read them.

The commonest, yet perhaps the most rarely mastered of the arts is communication through the word. I only hope I have written with sufficient skill and feeling to enable you, dear reader, to get out of my words a half of what I want them to mean. Then the book must be worth your while, and I shall have triumphed.

A Word About
the Case Histories

THE LIFE STORIES of criminals and of the famous can be bought by the pound or obtained free at a good public library; but bona fide histories of typical law-abiding people are hard to come by. The reason is that ordinary citizens are not forced to give their *true* histories to anybody, and they have no desire to do so. If they do agree to tell all, they can be expected to hold back certain key information anyway, on the ground that it is nobody's business but their own. Yet, in my book, I wanted to use the histories of everyday people to sharpen some of my points.

What to do?

My solution has been to use the arts of the storyteller to fabricate some of my case histories, but not all of them, taking as my basis a vast amount of government data, studies published by social scientists, and my own observations. I would not have been obliged to resort to this stratagem if I had chosen to confine my cases to those of braggarts, famous people and circus performers, and if I had been willing to settle for such information as these people would give me. It is precisely because I wanted truth in depth, and because I could not limit myself to wonderful and famous personalities, that I have had to use some fiction to light up the truths in this book.

In a deep sense, and except for the case of Meyer Mueller, these are studies from life as it is lived in the United States today; for fiction is often truer than truth itself. Bearing this in mind, the reader should not be surprised to find that he has a cousin or neighbor much like someone he will meet in these pages.

Yet not everybody in this book is fictional. Three of my many flesh-and-blood guests are Clarence B. Randall, P. G. Wodehouse, and Richard Rodgers. The identities of most of the other living persons are concealed, as by change of name, change of place of residence, and so forth.

The Way In

LIFE BEGINS AT FIFTY is a mind-stretching, get-ready book for quinquagenarians who would like to know where they are going and would prefer to have a little fun on the way. It suggests, by turn playfully and seriously, how male and female denizens of the second half century can look their problems in the eye and still have something close to a maximum of pleasure.

The pleasure-mad reader of these pages can congratulate himself on his good fortune in having a hedonist as his guide to a more amusing life. A hedonist, you know, is a fellow who gets so much pleasure out of fun that he looks for it most of the time, and always tries to avoid its opposite, which is unfun. So you might say I am practically a Coney Island guide.

Life begins at fifty. Because I accept this thesis, the book in your hand does not hold to the view that the years from fifty to sixty-five should be spent in dull preparation for life thereafter, or in the hereafter. But even Coney Island has its flat stretches as well as its roller coasters, and I fear you may find my book dull at times. To be honest, furthermore, I had better confess quickly that between the dullness and the laughter you may find an occasional tear trickling down the whiskers or rinsing off the make-up.

Along with the dull pages and the tears and the laughter there is also a good measure of vital information ripped roasting hot from the seared pages of the *Statistical Abstract of the United States,* 83d edition. Here, indeed, is no joke. We are born, we play, we laugh, we suffer, we love, we work, we die.

The government and various universities and foundations have caused the numerical representations of our private joys and miseries to be gathered together in the *Statistical Abstract* and thousands of other books, articles, and pamphlets. I have taken some of these representations, added some true and some fictional case histories, some personal philosophy, a touch of P. G. Wodehouse, salt, pepper and tabasco sauce, and here serve up the result for your delectation, together with a side dish of spiced digressions. If you do not relish the facts, maybe you will enjoy the flavoring.

In writing my book, then, I have drawn on personal observations and on the testimony of many people. I have examined many a government report replete with figures and footnotes; and, as if all this were not enough, I have for years been scanning newspapers, magazines and medical journals for odd tidbits of information that might shed a little light into some cranny overlooked by the specialists.

Through all this effort I picked up more information than I wanted, and I acquired a broader view of my subject than I had thought possible a mere two years ago, when I was already a full year into my research.

At first I thought I would be writing a book of simple encouragement for middle-aged Man. Then, like Adam wakening from a deep sleep, I discovered Woman; having found her, I found sex, too (although I still have not found any sin). I learned that Woman, at fifty and beyond, has her own unhappiness as well as her happiness. I learned that, while some of her unhappinesses are hers alone (just as Man has some that are only his), there are others that she shares with the male of the species. Then came the discovery that fifty-year-old Man and fifty-year-old Woman can often find happiness together—a finding which reminded me of a quite similar revelation that came upon me in my youth.

An excess of knowledge and my new understanding have vastly complicated my task of writing. In my book the simple middle-aged man is no longer simple, and he is often not middle-aged. As I point out later, some men of fifty are young men, while others are old enough to be your uncle; something similar can be said of fifty-year-old women. The plain fact is that individuals of the age simply refuse to fit in with the nice, handy generalizations which are the coin of the social sciences. I don't claim this makes the generalizations useless; it isn't quite that bad. The fact is, though, that like people of a younger age, your fifty-year-old comes in different shapes, sizes, colors, religions, dispositions and sexes. Some are healthy, some are wealthy, some are neither. Among the fifty-year-olds there are plenty of the crusty, the kind, the somber, and the funny. There are strong men and weak men, aggressive women and meek women, cold people and feverish people.

A lot of these so-various people are on the right track, so far as I can tell. Others are headed for trouble, but can avoid it if they will only try. A number are in trouble now and will have to do some vigorous head-scratching before they get out of it.

What of the things we face in common? Each of us, we believe, will die before reaching the age of 120—although Charlie Smith, according to the Social Security Administration, did not. If I'm wrong that all of us must fail where Mr. Smith succeeded, so much the better. Then there are the glacial changes. We age biologically, for one thing, and have been doing so since birth. We become more self-centered (not always a bad thing). Our judgment improves (always a good thing). Yes, thank heaven, there are some valid generalizations—even some pleasant ones.

Let us now, merely as an exercise, consider the number fifty as a number of miles and as a temperature in the shade, and finally as an age in the life of man.

A man who has swum fifty miles has been in the water a long, long time. He has come an exceedingly long distance, is very tired, and has achieved the nearly impossible. In a jet plane, on the other hand, fifty miles may be covered in five minutes, the time it takes to ride a New York subway from 28th Street to 50th Street. Fifty miles whisk by every ten seconds when you are in an earth satellite. So if fifty miles is infinity to the swimmer, it is a trifle to the jet pilot, and a thirtieth of a trifle to an orbiter.

A July temperature of fifty in the shade would chill the bone marrow; but let January temperatures in Minneapolis, Boston, or New York reach fifty for three days running and reporters will be out scouring the parks for signs of premature pussy willows. So fifty degrees Fahrenheit can be very cold or very warm. Is this a commonplace? My apologies!

To a child of six, an age of fifty years is inconceivable. To a twenty-year-old, it is old age; to thirty and to seventy it is middle age; to an eighty-year-old it is youth. Clarence B. Randall's book *Sixty-Five Plus* opens with the words, "When a young man in business approaches fifty he becomes self-conscious about his age."

Until the middle of the present century fifty was a very old age in India, where life expectancy at birth had been only thirty-two years. Now the situation there has changed drastically, with life expectancy being extended almost a year every year in the late nineteen fifties and early sixties.

In 1900 the average American could look forward at birth to forty-seven years of life. Obviously, fifty was at that time a rather round, plump number—not quite so impressive as in India today, but awesome nevertheless. Now it is much less so. At birth, today's well-informed American infant knows he can expect to live to the age of seventy. So, fifty has shrunk drastically from the way we saw it in India, and impressively from the way it recently appeared in the United States. It shrinks some more if we examine it from the standpoint of today's fifty-year-old American, who can expect to live to the age of seventy-five. (At sixty-five, furthermore, he will expect to reach seventy-nine. Generally, white males and nonwhites do not do quite as well as these figures indicate, while white women top the given figures by two to three years.)

A cornerstone of the philosophy underlying this book is that fifty is a flexible, adjustable age, which people make younger or older, depending on who they are and on what they want of it. Some who are fifty groan with terror. Vainly they wish they were younger. When they dye their hair, they do not succeed in making fifty seem anything significantly less than a hundred. For what matters most (although they won't admit it) is how old they *really* are, in their minds and in their bodies, not how old some stranger on the other side of the street thinks they may be.

Luckily, there are many of both sexes for whom the age of fifty holds no fear. Like everybody today these people must occasionally write their ages on passport applications and such documents. Seeing the nice round number they have written, they shake their heads and smile. Fifty years old, one such man thinks to himself: Holy Goboly! I'm a real old-timer. He looks up and catches the eye of a clerk standing nearby. "A hundred years old today," he says.

"Yeah, I could tell to look at you," the clerk replies. Privately, he is amused. This isn't the first time he has seen one of these guys nearing forty who thinks he is already older than God; still, it's always pretty funny.

This man who says he is a hundred just does not know how to 'act his age' of fifty. He is neither afraid nor bowed. If you knew him, you might sense something indecent about his frivolity. He is probably getting a lot more fun out of his family, his job, his pet projects, his hobbies and his sex life than a man of his age ought to. What can be done about such an irresponsible fellow, anyway? Should he be denounced to the House Committee on Un-American Activities?

Suppose the Committee launches an investigation into this man's un-American merriment. What will it discover? First, of course, it will reach a typical Committee finding: The subject is a large one requiring extended hearings; hundreds of witnesses will have to be called; large amounts of taxpayers' money must be expended.

Soon the Committee will discover that it cannot make much headway against our friend without first finding out what the age limits are for youth, middle age and old age. Early in the proceedings it will be noticed that witnesses are giving conflicting testimony on this question. There will even be rumors that some are to be held in contempt of Congress.

An advertising man who uses only teen-age models in his ads will swear that Youth ends at twenty-four, and that Old Age begins at thirty.

An executive of an organization that supervises corporate retirement plans will swear under oath that it does not matter when Youth ends or when Middle Age begins, and that nobody has determined, clinically, when these events occur. On the other hand, he will solemnly depose that Old Age begins at sixty-five, when his pension plans invariably take over.

A former beauty queen, now in her fifties, will state that there is no such thing as Middle Age, that Old Age begins as soon as Youth ends, "and I hope not to live so long."

She will be replaced in the witness chair by a woman somewhere between thirty and eighty who, in response to all questions relating to age, will take the Fifth Amendment, on the ground that her answers might tend to incriminate her.

The next to last witness, I predict, will be a man in his twenties, crippled in an automobile accident three years ago, who will be helped into the chair by a trained nurse. He will swear that Old Age begins as soon as you are smashed up good.

The very last witness, a man of eighty-nine who seized control of a vast corporation when he was eighty, and has since tripled its holdings, will testify under oath that he is not old, and that while he does not understand old age, he is positive it is something God has invented to occupy the vestigial brains of fools and suckers.

I foresee that when the evidence is all in, the Committee will deliberate long and confusedly. At last it will issue a two-thousand-page report that will suggest that old age sets in at various times in different people (which it does), that more and more people are getting un-American, and that all of the witnesses were unreliable if not downright untruthful. The man who started the trouble by saying he was a hundred when he seemed forty (and was actually fifty) will long since have been forgotten. With a sigh of relief, the Committee will turn back to its time-honored job of asking college boys whether Fidel Castro's beard is longer than Karl Marx's, or how many Committee members can dance on the head of a pin.

When my father wrote *Life Begins at Forty* he started several things at once. Probably the least of these was that he launched a famous best seller, the popularity of which has become legend.

He also orbited an idea that has already outlived his book by a good twenty-five years. His idea—that there is a wonderfully worthwhile life that begins in middle age, if we will only let it—was something new under the sun, and it quickly became a popular notion.

So it was that "life begins at forty" passed into the language, and became a truism of middle age. It was later used on countless greeting cards, it was the title of a movie starring Will Rogers, it was given a Broadway twist to help put over a show called *Life Begins at Eight-Forty,* and it has been borrowed as the title of a column in the Hearst newspapers.

Something else that Walter B. Pitkin started with his book was the whole industry that has grown up around the popular, inspirational, self-help book. For *Life Begins at Forty* was a pioneer in its field. Without it, and without some of my father's other books of the twenties and thirties, a hundred well-known authors of a generation, and a thousand books, would have wound up exactly where Alice, of *Alice in Wonderland,* would be today if there had been no Lewis Carroll. I confess I don't know where that is.

Life Begins at Forty had another, more important influence. It brought attention to *the subjective, or inner life* of the middle-aged and aging person. By suggesting the promise of a challenging, creative, happy life-after-youth, the book did much to open the door for the field of medical practice known as geriatrics and for gerontology, which is the study of aging. Medicine had long been interested in the prolongation of life, and social workers realized what a problem dependent old people can be in low-income families. But it took something new and different to awaken America to the fact that the huge slice of life left after forty is indeed life and includes, for many of us, much of the best of it.

While present-day geriatrics is concerned with the aging person, it is not only trying to add a few weeks, months or years to life. The geriatrician tries to promote good health and life adjustment. To do this, he helps his patients combat various ailments, and he resorts to a wide range of life-saving techniques. But in the end his aim, as a specialist, is to raise the tone of life-after-youth.

In the Soviet Union geriatrics is something else again. There the aim is also to prolong life and, especially, to extend the portion of life during which people can be socially productive. But perhaps the Russian brand is not so different from ours as it appears. For an older person who is good at his job must be capable of living a good life.

Most, but not quite all, of what followed from *Life Begins at Forty* was good. I think the worst results were the cheery books and magazine articles that informed the reader that growing old is merely a bright, sunny experience, rather similar to a midwinter vacation in the Virgin Islands. All this printed goo would not have been such a bad thing if it were not that, with some timely thought and effort, we can make our later years enjoyable and even exciting. I will go farther: Many people can enjoy retirement *only* if they think ahead and prepare for it.

The shame is that so many of the cheery, soft-headed books and articles have encouraged the reader to relax at the very time when he should be thinking and working toward his later goals. And heaven help him if he has no goals and cannot invent any. The much-discussed problem of the high-school dropout is nothing compared with that of the *life* dropout of sixty.

During the nineteen fifties it was repeatedly suggested to me that I should revise and update my father's book. Because the subject intrigued me, I started to look into the idea. To my chagrin I quickly discovered that the book was so personal in its terms, and so dated, that no mere revision could make it appropriate to today's needs. The only solution was to write a new book, and the more I thought about that, the more convinced I became that the problem now, and the opportunity, too, centered around the age of fifty, not forty.

For times have changed. In 1932, when *Life Begins at Forty* was written, the fortieth birthday caused cold shivers to run along the spine. Life expectancy at birth then was sixty years. Today it is seventy. In those days to lose a job as one neared forty might be catastrophic. Today we are more advanced economically, socially and medically, and the total prospect from the age of fifty is now superior to the prospect from forty a generation ago.

Even so, if forty was the age that made people quake then, fifty, as one man put it to me, is the crusher today. Not that society discards the fifty-year-old! Most often the trouble seems to be that men and women of fifty experience a loss of purpose or direction. To some, this aimlessness is so frightening that, like the proverbial ostrich, they bury their heads in the sand. They hear no evil, see no evil, speak no evil; but what they think is nobody's business.

A little fright can be a good thing, provided it spurs us to face reality and to deal with it as rational beings. While there is literally no escape from aging, this side of the grave, happiness awaits the man who will seek knowledge—and then act on it. Here it is well to recall a fact known to psychologists, that action is the sworn enemy of fear. As we shall see, the active person in his second half century has little need to fear the future.

There are good reasons for reading up on life after fifty. One reason is the widespread feeling that there is something strange, something almost weird, about the second half century. To some who are fifty, it is as if all of life were included in one of those ancient charts, wherein the mapmaker drew the borders of the known countries boldly and precisely. The remote areas of the New World, being unknown to him, he sketched in lightly and filled with monsters and representations of frigid blasts from arctic regions unknown. Toward the lower left-hand corner he inserted the Fountain of Youth. To our fifty-year-old, the boldly drawn lands represent the known ages up to the half century, while the monster-peopled wastes and dimly perceived wildernesses are that part of life lying off in the future.

The first reason, then, may be the reader's hope that some book or article will tell him whether the dragons are real, whether the trip over the ocean is unduly hazardous, what the New World is really like, what work is to be done there. This reason is the need for comfort; it is not the comfort of the soothsayer, the priest or the politician one seeks, but the comfort of knowledge, which can convert a looming, unknown evil into a lesser, known evil, or even into a friendly elf or gnome. In more philosophical terms, the reader may hope that a book will tell him something about the meaning of life beyond the half century.

Secondly, he may look for the pithy, practical points with which do-it-yourself books are usually so crammed. Possibly he wants to know the ins and outs of frolicking at fifty, of sex at sixty, of sun-bathing and salt-free diets at seventy, of eating at eighty, and of nibbling at ninety. He may seek guidance about money, health, housing, places to retire to, occupations for the elderly, hobbies, relations with his offspring and his offspring's offspring, and so on.

Then there is a third reason. It is the hope that a book or article may shed some light on the chances of attaining continued usefulness, continued independence of mind and spirit, continued self-fulfillment. For at all stages of life, short of senility, we require more than security, more than creature comforts, more than kindness. We also need purpose, challenge, direction, even conflict. The fact that each of us needs these in different degrees, and in different shapes, in no way lessens our dependence on them. For without these normal stimuli we languish; our mental powers and even our bodies decay with unnecessary swiftness.

This book does not contain inside tips on where to retire to or on what precise diets or medicines to seek out. Medical and other counseling services must meet these needs. Here, on the other hand, you will find some informing light on those far seas and distant continents whose mysteries may have goaded your curiosity or made your hackles rise. Here, too, are one man's strongly held convictions about a host of matters relating to self-fulfillment after fifty.

In recent decades too much has been assumed about the necessity for people past their twenties to adjust to a youth-centered American culture. In these pages I project a non-youth-centered world, in which the mature wield increasing power over their own multiple destinies—by knowing what they want and going after it. Surely if older people are to get into the main stream of American life, which is where at least one writer says they already are, it will be because they put themselves there, one at a time, through their own efforts.

Yet the main stream may not always be the best place to be. Shady brooks and quiet tributaries have charms unknown to the muddy Mississippi.

Beyond aging and age (Who cares, after all, about age? What does it matter? It is who and what you are, how you use your head, and what you do, that count in this world!), this is a book about work and play and leisure and books and sexual relations. It touches lightly on Richard Rodgers, Adolf Hitler, some salespeople in a Chicago department store, a man who knows linoleum from A to Z, the Carolina Parakeet (which never adjusted to apple orchards and is therefore extinct), some steelworkers, and quite a few others. Despite the parakeet, the book is concerned mostly with people and with the quality of humanity. I suppose it is, therefore, a vulgar book.

Vulgar or not, in these pages we do not mindlessly applaud gray hair; nor do we cure it; nor do we lament it; nor do we ignore it. We recognize it as a condition of nature and try to work with it as Frank Lloyd Wright knew so well how to work with a piece of hilly land.

Any Hawkshaw among my readers will be able to pick out some spots where I have allowed my imagination to take over. At only one or two points do I give the reader advance warning that we are about to soar off together into the bright, blue yonder; and so he is advised to keep his eyes peeled for anything that has the look of mind run riot. In any case I can assure him that I have not cheated. Not once do I credit the *Statistical Abstract* for something I have invented.

Have you ever gone into a big hardware store and been struck by the variety of items on display there? Or have you ever wondered why so many book titles have to be carried in stock by even a medium-size book store? There are big books, little books, fat books, skinny books, short books, tall books, red books, green books—and all the books with different names outside are different inside, too. Isn't it amazing what a variety of books old Mr. Gutenberg's printing press can turn out?

Still, there is at least one thing we all see every day that is more various than the tools in the hardware store or the books in the biggest book shop, and that is the people who buy them. People come in different ages, heights, colors, weights, national backgrounds, and religions. Some are married, some are single, some are divorced, some are widowed. Yet, different as people are, we can easily see a number of things that groups of them have in common. Consider place of residence: Many people live in cities; others in towns; others in suburban neighborhoods; others in the country; others on little boats anchored off Hong Kong. Or take broad types of occupation: The biggest employed groups are the housewives and the school children; beyond these there are the owners of businesses, the executives, other business employees, the so-called blue-collar workers, the retired, the unemployed, and many others.

Or consider age: Right now there is a group of people aged one minute, another group aged two minutes, another three minutes, and so on, all the way up to more minutes than anyone could count in three months.

Despite the tens and hundreds of thousands of individual and group differences, there is one cord that ties us all together as neatly as a ribbon around a little bundle of kindling sold in a New York store at Christmastime. This cord is our common strain of humanity. An obvious fact, you might say, and hardly worth mentioning; yet our essential humanity is forgotten every day by policemen who treat teen-age boys like dogs, by hack writers of published short stories whose characters are cut out of paper, and—what especially concerns us here—by writers of nonfiction who treat people of various types and ages as if they were distinct kinds of animals. But the human animal is all one animal, my friends.

An error at the root of much of the writing and thinking on the subject of middle age and old age is the notion that these segments of life are very unlike the earlier parts of our existence. In fact, life after fifty is strikingly like life at thirty. It is, after all, *life;* that is what counts most. As such, it may partake of more or less sexuality, more or less family pleasure and responsibility, more or less work, more or less anxiety, more or less philosophy. Of course, there *are* typical differences between people of different ages; I point these out repeatedly in these pages.

Infinitely more profound than the sum of the differences, however, are the likenesses that persist all through life. More basic than change, more important than aging, are the obvious continuities such as that all our lives our bones are clad in flesh, that that flesh is fed by a stream of blood constantly heated to a temperature of 98.6 when measured at the mouth, that our eyes gauge the distance of objects through the phenomenon of parallax, and that our brains direct and coordinate our conscious actions.

So it is that I write here of humanity and of happiness and of the common human experience, and not merely of what may chance to happen at one time. I ask the reader to remember this when he comes to the case of a nameless John Doe, age fifty, or a named John Smith, age fifty-five. The particular cases are here to help us understand the general condition; the generalizations are here to help us see our own particular cases.

This is a new book, for a new age. What it contains is, I believe, particularly appropriate for North Americans, West Europeans and Australians. But above all, it is for those of fifty and more years, no matter where they dwell, who are curious enough to want to think about difficulties as well as fun, futures, opportunities and ideas. As you see, it is not a chauvinistic book. Even those under fifty may read it, if they wish.

When we were twenty, our lives had become our own, and the world was our oyster. I say here that when we are fifty our lives are our own, and the world is our oyster.

I hope the reader enjoys the oyster as much as I do.

The View
from the Fiftieth Floor

FOR TENS OF THOUSANDS OF YEARS, since before the invention of the wheel, man has been struggling for knowledge and for mastery of his world. Each new discovery and each new mechanical device has been passed down from father to son, so that, with few exceptions, every age has been better informed and technologically more advanced than the age before it. Each step forward rests on the ingenuity of men long dead. Without Arabic numbers, including the concept of the cipher (0), Einstein might have been a sorcerer's apprentice and the general theory of relativity might still be waiting for a Congolese mathematician of the year 5000. Any delay in the invention of the wheel might have put off the discovery of penicillin and of the inner workings of the atom, unrelated as these fields of knowledge may seem.

Modern man has used his heritage of information to probe into the secrets of the universe and of the human mind and body. His judgment is almost as suspect as ever, for this he cannot inherit as he can the contents of a textbook; but his knowledge of himself and of the physical world around him have outraced the weirdest dreams of a generation ago.

Thus today's men and women of fifty are heirs to history's richest store of knowledge, the beneficiaries of the greatest treasure known to our kind. But if much of the hoard in our bulging cornucopia originated deep in history, other portions are the product of our own individual labors within the past half century.

You who are fifty gain more from your own past than younger people do, because your past is so much longer and richer than theirs. From your personal history you have gained judgment and insight and knowledge that youth lacks. Indeed, judgment comes to us only with age and commonly improves beyond the Biblical three score and ten years.

It follows that the background of a person of fifty fits him to deal with human problems more surely and with less effort than ever before, and more confidently and better than those who are younger. How wasteful the labors of those still under thirty seem as they try this, that, and the other scheme to get something done—something which the fifty-year-old could do so easily if he had to!

Then, too, you who are fifty have likely found that you are more favorably situated than most young people you know. Having accumulated some hard assets over a number of years, you should be financially better off than they are, on the average, and being farther along in life, you have likely discharged a number of obligations and finished chores which still tie down those who are forty and less. For example, you will probably never again have to change a diaper, never again have to hire a baby sitter, never again have to dance a jig or a tarantella when the boss snaps his fingers.* Younger men are taking over the harder, less rewarding jobs, in the office and on the road. Younger women have taken on the P.T.A. grind.

Does all this sound too rosy? Does life begin at fifty for everybody? Not by a long shot. In fact, most of Earth's people still do not live to see their fiftieth birthday, and there are millions born each year who will be healthy at twenty— and dead before thirty. Life surely does not begin at fifty for the multitudes who live well beyond that age, but are so poor

* A slow waltz will do now.

they still must labor from dawn until after dark just for shelter and a little bread and cheese. Again, life does not begin at fifty for many whose physical or mental health is seriously impaired, though it is nonetheless true that some of the disabled make surprising adjustments that enable them to live happily to an advanced age. Among those for whom the circumstances of birth and environment make 'fifty' and 'old' synonymous would be perhaps a quarter of all Americans, a third of West Europeans, and upwards of nine tenths of Latin Americans, Asians and Africans.

The above exceptions are what we might call the honest casualties. The willful casualties are another kind of exception; these are the chronic soreheads, who expect too little from this world, and therefore get less—a fact which, to them, neatly justifies their sour attitude. There are also those with so little ability to arrange their lives that at fifty they have become mere drifters. For some, life is over at fifty, because their dim minds define life only as animality. Lacking the will to break out of a deadly rhythm of eating, sleeping and working (for whatever financial reward), they plow endlessly downward until at last they are six feet under the sod. The age at which they arrive there need not concern us here.

Self-pity is not rare at fifty. But from at least one limited, grim point of view, our lot on earth, at any age, is not so wonderful that by contrast those past fifty have any special claim to pity. Who would be the chief losers if mankind were to be cut off by a series of beautiful, bright flashes beginning at 9:26 tonight? The answer is easy: The big losers would be the young, who have had so little chance to understand what life is about or to savor its deeper pleasures. Weep, if you must, for the young, for they stand most in need of life.

The broodings of the postfifty are commonly misdirected. Too often healthy physical change is mistaken for rapid decline, ordinary ill-health is taken for disaster. Sickness needing prompt diagnosis and attention may go unrecognized, because the sufferer imagines his trouble is only his age— or, in appropriately corny terms, that 'his number is up.'

Those who have their health, and are nevertheless filled with self-pity, might stop to ask whether their case is as sad as that of the child of twelve whose parents are going broke, or whose marriage is shattered; or as sad as the case of the seventeen-year-old who yearns to get into a good college and learns he cannot; or nearly as sad as the case of the physically broken mother of three young children whose husband walks out on her; or as sad as the case of the twenty-eight-year-old accountant who is going blind; or as utterly miserable as the case of the billion human beings (give or take a hundred million) whose health is wrecked beyond repair before they reach forty.

A further perspective for today's fortunate fifty-year-olds is that provided by comparing today's Americans with those of 1900. Today three quarters of our quinquagenarians have the resources to enjoy life, while in 1900 perhaps only a third of the farmers and a tenth of the nonfarmers could do so; the rest had scant savings, no provisions for retirement, no job security, and often too little strength or will to live after a lifetime battle for survival.

The increase in man-hour productivity and in the size of the national and international neighborhoods in which we freely move, the leveling of the great antisocial fortunes combined with the arrival of Social Security and other types of insurance, the huge advances in medicine, housing, and transportation, the perfection of gadgets like the vacuum cleaner and washing machine—all these things and many others have given present-day Americans a degree of physical mobility and security and a kind of freedom our grandfathers never knew.

What a tremendous improvement this suggests! How little room it leaves for self-pity! What a challenge it poses for those among the lucky three quarters who have the will to make life more pleasurable and more meaningful than ever before.

Much of history has labored to bring our world to the high level of health and intellectual richness and productivity it has now attained. We perceive, too, that much of our youth was spent in toil to raise us to whatever levels of wisdom and material wealth each of us has found. And now younger people, more zestful perhaps, but less knowledgeable than we are, and lacking in judgment, are performing the meaner tasks we have left behind.

The world is at your feet. What will you do with it? Here, I believe, is the great question for those who have an immediate personal interest in our subject. At birth, what we were to become depended first on what we were, that is, on our physical inheritance; then on what people would do to us and for us; and lastly on what we would do on our own account. The same is true fifty years later, though the emphasis has shifted dramatically. For now the stress is all on what we may elect to do for ourselves.

At twenty, more or less, a young man or woman is supposed to decide what he is to be. It is an illusion that at our age we are no longer capable of making such a decision. At fifty we can still decide whether to be earth-bound or airborne, whether to be followers or leaders, whether to be producers or leeches, whether to be creators, spectators or doers, whether to suffer silently or to celebrate noisily. Believe it or not, many of us can and do decide to change our careers after fifty; but that is easier said than done.

If American life expectancy at birth in this century has been raised from forty-seven to seventy years, and if gerontologists and geriatricians are rapidly learning about aging and what to do for it and with it, is there any prospect that American infants will have a life expectancy of eighty-five or ninety years in the year 2000? And in the year 2200 will life-insurance policies be written on the basis of an expectancy of 150 or more? Suppose the answers are Yes. Would the masses then enjoy that part of life which lies beyond ninety or 150 years?

What miracles would have to be passed if all these wish-thoughts were to take the shape of reality, so that millions aged 150 or more might live interesting and active lives? Or are no miracles necessary, that is to say, won't medical science, given time, bring these things to pass anyway?

We do not know the answers. They are riddles hidden in a future that is beyond us and our sketchy knowledge—sketchy, that is, by comparison with what will be known in the year 2200, or even in 1980. But it is interesting that among life-scientists now seeking the answers there are those who believe that the elimination of certain standard causes of death, such as cancer and the circulatory ailments, might theoretically produce a society in which all would live through the twelfth decade—and then gently expire. Not everybody agrees, but among the dissenters I know of no respected American authority who holds that large numbers may one day live past 120. For, as we shall see in another chapter, there really is such a thing as aging, and there are quite a few anatomical and other symptoms of it aside from the known effects of sickness. To date there is no solid basis for belief that these anatomical and physiological symptoms will ever be conquered, even though some deferment cannot be ruled out.

Yet it is clear that over the next several decades life expectancy will continue to rise, and I confidently predict the day will come when a New York publisher will issue a book called *Life Begins at Seventy*. For such a volume to be seriously put forth, two sets of conditions will first have to be met:

1. Average life expectancy at birth will have to be close to ninety, as against seventy today. At seventy, the

average person should expect to live to not less than ninety-five, against today's eighty-one. For this to happen, medical science must bring to heel at least one of the major circulatory or degenerative diseases. Life's later years must also become more vigorous. Nowadays too few of those past seventy-five are able to pursue any occupation to advantage.

2. Our antiquated employment and retirement laws and practices must be overhauled. Employers will no longer retire the worker merely because he has reached sixty-five, but will do so only because the employee requests retirement (being entitled to it) or because he can no longer earn his keep. Pension and old-age insurance plans, including Social Security, will contain built-in safeguards against inflation.

So there will have to be a medical and a social revolution before *Life Begins at Seventy* can appear. Like the revolution in medicine, the social revolution will add years to life. It will do this by making life after sixty-five more worth living for millions who, given a chance to work, would prefer not to retire. These people—who admittedly do not include nearly all the healthy men who today retire at sixty-five—will have an increased will to live. Given the will, the way will be found, within limits.

But, for the next few decades, perhaps until about 1990 (which is no more remote from the time I write this than is the year 1938), we had better try to get along with the notion that life begins at fifty—or at most sixty. Not such a bad idea, when you think about it!

Life at all ages is uncertain, and it is in this regard that it differs so happily from death. Life begins, as we know, when we set off on some great adventure the outcome of which is in doubt. Our birth is such an adventure, and so is our education. Marriage and the beginning of a career bear the same proud hallmarks of adventure and uncertainty. What a wonderful thing that life after fifty can be filled with adventure, too, even if the uncertainty of life itself must still travel by adventure's side!

Sermon in Favor of Fun

THE MESSAGE of these pages will be missed if the reader takes them all so seriously that henceforth he spends his free hours trying to follow some supposed prescription for living found here. People and the circumstances of their lives vary too widely for any such formula to be taken literally. Consider laughter, surely an important activity, and often thought to be essential to contentment. Yet I know a man who seems happier than most; he has an excellent sense of humor too, but *he never laughs*. How can we allow for his glum visage in a formula that sets laughter up as a *sine qua non* of happiness?

Yet if there *is* a sure-fire prescription it must include fun and merriment; for there is much too much seriousness in life for it all to be taken without spice or flavoring. So, let us now consider the proposition that fun is the great imperative of life.

I have a friend who says we all have a duty to make as much money as possible. Without now disputing him, I say it is a higher duty of every man, woman and corporation to have fun. There are many serious arguments for this, as we shall see.

But first we will have to get our definition straight. What is "fun" anyway? Not having a television pundit such as Bergen Evans at my elbow to enlighten me, I have looked the entries up in *Webster's Third New International Dictionary*. Here is what I found:

¹fun \'fən\ vb funned; funned; funning; funs ᴌpern. aiter.
of ME fonnen to fool, make a fool of, fr. fonne fool, dupe] vt,
now dial : HOAX, TEASE, TRICK, KID ~ vi [fr. ²fun] : to
indulge in banter or play : speak or act in fun : JOKE, FOOL
⟨funning about the marriage⟩ ⟨passed the time funning till
others tired of his horseplay⟩
²fun \"\ n -s 1 obs : a practical joke : TRICK, HOAX 2 : what
provides amusement or enjoyment ⟨a book that is ~ to read⟩
⟨a fellow who is ~ to have around⟩ : enjoyable activity ⟨the
game was no ~⟩ ⟨picnics are great ~⟩ ⟨didn't know hard study
could be so much ~⟩ ⟨sitting on the ground was part of the
~⟩; specif : playful often boisterous action or speech : JOCU-
LARITY : RIDICULE ⟨made myself a fine figure of ~ for someone
outside —Arthur Grimble⟩ 3 : the disposition or mood to
find or make a cause for amusement : PLAYFULNESS ⟨a carefree man who was always full of ~⟩ ⟨has a lot of ~ in him⟩
⟨don't say that even in ~⟩ 4 : AMUSEMENT, ENJOYMENT
⟨play cards for ~⟩ ⟨have ~ at the party⟩ ⟨the baby had a lot
of ~ with the blocks⟩ ⟨robbed him just for the ~ of it⟩
⟨never got any ~ out of listening to serious music⟩ 5 : violent
or excited activity or argument : FIREWORKS ⟨a rabbit stam-
peded the herd and then the ~ began⟩ ⟨just toss in the South
as a conversation piece and watch the ~ —James Street⟩
  syn FUN, JEST, SPORT, GAME, and PLAY agree in designating
what provides diversion or amusement or is intended to
arouse laughter. FUN implies amusement or an engagement in
what interests as an end in itself or applies to what provides
this amusement or interest, often also implying a propensity
for laughing or for finding a usu. genial cause for laughter or
amusement ⟨had such a zest for everything and thought it all
such fun —O.E.Rölvaag⟩ ⟨make living more fun, life more
complete —Printers' Ink⟩ ⟨a man full of fun⟩ JEST occurs in
phrases (as in jest) or applies to activity or utterance not to be
taken seriously, sometimes carrying an implication of ridicule
or hoaxing ⟨a man given to making his most significant re-
marks in jest⟩ ⟨make jest of very serious problems⟩ SPORT,
often interchangeable with FUN ⟨there is a good deal of sport in
many serious activities⟩ or JEST ⟨play a trick on a friend for
the sport of it⟩ or GAME, although here usu. generic or applying
to activity calling for a certain skill ⟨go at sport as if it were a
way of life⟩ ⟨the sport of fly casting⟩ ⟨the sport of tennis⟩ can
also imply amusement or provoking of laughter by putting
someone or something up to gentle or malicious ridicule
⟨make sport of a suggestion⟩ ⟨make a good deal of sport out of
someone else's misfortune⟩ GAME in a now rare earlier sense of
FUN implies a certain ridicule ⟨make game of an unfortunate
rival⟩ More commonly today it applies to any activity engaged
in for fun ⟨a game of tennis⟩ ⟨games to keep children amused⟩
PLAY, a generic term for all games or amusements, stresses in
all senses an opposition to earnest, carrying no suggestion of
anything but an intent to divert or be diverted ⟨play time in a
nursery⟩ ⟨made his work play by enjoying it thoroughly⟩
⟨pretend to spank a child in play⟩
³fun \"\ adj [²fun] 1 : providing fun, entertainment, or
amusement ⟨a ~ party⟩ ⟨~ hat⟩ 2 : full of fun : PLEASANT
⟨a ~ night⟩ ⟨have a ~ time⟩
⁴fun \"\ n -s [alter. of whin] Scot : FURZE
⁵fun \'fün, -üŋ\ n, pl fun [Jap] : a Japanese unit of weight
equal to ¹⁄₁₀ momme, .375 grams, or 5.79 grains

To come to grips, let us first get rid of the definitions that
do not concern us. How about ¹**fun?** No, this is not for us,
because it is a *vb,* and we need a *n*—quick. Out with it! Then
³**fun** is a lowly (and, I might add, questionable) adjective.
Out! Now ⁴**fun** and ⁵**fun** are at least nouns; but what do they

mean, pray? One is furze and the other is 1/10 of a momme. Furze we don't need, it being a warm day, and why settle for a tenth part of a momme when so many mommies with all their parts are always eager for a good time? Out, out, out!

This leaves us with ²**fun,** another noun, which the dictionary breaks down into divisions **1, 2, 3, 4,** and **5.** To save time, let's chuck **1, 3,** and **5** right away. Definition **2** is worth remembering: "what provides amusement or enjoyment (a book that is fun to read) . . ." etc. Number **4** is more useful: "AMUSEMENT, ENJOYMENT (play cards for ⌣) . . . (robbed him just for the ⌣ of it)" and so on. This almost hits the nail on the head, but not quite, because the subject of our sermon is delight in small doses, and not such long-drawn-out pleasures as a lazy trip up the Amazon or to Italy and into the crater of Vesuvius when in eruption. That might be highly amusing, but it would hardly be fun.

Fun is a joke, a pun, an hour or two at the right movie, a game of ping-pong, or a roll in the hay. It is whiskey with friends, it is a joke written at the bottom of a letter, and, as Hamlin Garland wrote, it is buying things for yourself. Many novels and a few funny books are fun to read. So are good mystery yarns and well-written biographies of rascals. This book is fun (if you agree, tell your friends right now, while you think of it; if you disagree, go tell your enemies what fun it is). Swimming in the ocean may be fun, and lying on the beach is a lazy kind of fun. Gambling can be fun; poker is often fun. Fishing is fun. Lots of things are fun. Choose your own brand and go to it.

As an Englishman has put it, fun is a giggle. But it is also a romp or a roll or a frolic or a gambol or even a gulp, if it be the right sort of gulp. In a nutshell—or better still, in a funnel—fun is fun.

The enemies of fun are everywhere. It is said, for example, that there are those who mean to fight female nudity in the movies down to the last square centimeter. Shocking, but true. And then there is the modern Britisher, Sir A. P. Herbert, who has written: "People must not do things for fun. We are not here for fun. There is no reference to fun in any Act of Parliament." Ominous portents, these words, foretelling God knows what!

Consider what a terrible state things would be in if fun were abolished. Here are just a few of the likely results:

Games such as poker, croquet, baseball, tiddlywinks, and puss in the corner would lose their appeal.

All night clubs, shooting galleries, skating rinks, bowlaramas, Las Vegases, race tracks, and sporting houses would go out of business.

All funny men would become bores.

One or two TV shows would be in danger of closing down; Hollywood magnates would be obliged to go back into the garment business.

Love-making, which would no longer be fun, would have to be required by law, just as the payment of income tax is today. (If love were left on a voluntary basis, there would have to be love-recruitment posters outside post offices and other government buildings. One such sign would surely say, "Uncle Sam wants YOU to make love!")

Add to these dreadful consequences the throwing out of work of millions whose jobs depend on fun, and you have in prospect a calamity that boggles the mind. Clearly, each of us has a duty to himself and to his country to have fun regularly and often. The alternative may well be the collapse of civilization as we know it, or, even worse, the enforcement of a gaggle of pro-fun laws by a swollen, power-crazed bureaucracy.

At this perilous time, each thoughtful citizen must ask himself the question, "What can I do for fun?" Certainly he should not make excuses for himself, as by saying, "I'm having my share of fun right now," or "I've got a wife and kids; why pick on me? Take the single men first." To the person who says he is already having fun, I say, "Go and have some more. Have a drink, play some cards, go to a good movie, swim in the ocean, climb a mountain, tickle your spouse, smoke a cigar. Surely there must be something more you can do for fun."

To the man who says he shouldn't be called upon to have fun, because he has a wife and children to support, I make reply: "George Washington had his Martha, and he gave himself to his country. Abraham Lincoln had a wife and three sons, and he gave himself to his country. Are you arguing, little man, that because you have a wife and kids you will not even emit a little giggle for the cause of liberty?"

Fun is not only a duty to one's country; it is also a necessity of life. Like vitamin B, it is required by people of all ages, from infancy to 120, after which age it does not much matter. The person of fifty (or almost any other age) who has a strong pulse and good lungs, but has no fun, is not alive; he exists only to pay income tax. If that's all he cares to do, I'll make a deal with him; he can pay my income tax while I have fun enough for both of us.

Our everyday work, even when we enjoy it, leaves us with tensions that can be relieved by frequent doses of fun. This is equally true for housewives, secretaries, blue-collar workers, clerks, actuaries, salesmen, professional people, and big cheeses. Rest and sleep are helpful, even necessary, but they do not serve the same purpose that fun does. To understand the different functions of sleep and fun, consider this familiar phenomenon: A person who is tense because of stresses connected with his job finds it difficult to fall asleep at night. As a result, he gets too little rest, and he starts off the next day dead beat. But if the same person has fun before bedtime, his tensions vanish, he sleeps soundly, and he wakes up refreshed in the morning. Indeed, fun maketh a ready man.

So bear in mind that fun is an important reducer of workaday jitters, and never confuse its ends with those of sleep. We can have fun almost anywhere, any time, but we generally have to do our sleeping in bed at night. Still, I should be the last to suggest we cannot also have fun in bed.

A little fun in the evening can turn a flop of a day into a so-so one, or it can make a smashing success of an otherwise average day. Most days are so-so; the power fun has to improve our lives should therefore be obvious.

Yet too much fun after a brilliant day is dangerous, like eating fine, ripe Camembert on Italian bread while listening to Boccherini and beholding the Grand Canyon. There is always the danger that it can make you forget what was really so good about the day. And contrary to Pitkin's Proven Principle No. 1, that there is always room for a little more fun, it is well to bear in mind that all fun and no work makes Jack a dull boy. When the Camembert starts coming out the ears, Jack, it's time to get back on the job.

We now see that, while fun can occasionally be carried to excess, it is nevertheless a duty, a necessity, yes, and even a pleasure. So don't overlook it, now or ever. The goblins'll get you if you do.

Dr. Pitkin's Second
and Much More Serious
Sermon on Fun

LET US BE SERIOUS. Let us look at two breadwinners who had better start having some fun if they know what's good for them.

First our all-seeing eye comes to bear on Oliver Oakley, who got on the road to success in 1939 at the age of twenty-nine, when he went to work for his father-in-law's business of converting raw paper into scores of the various items sold in stationery stores. Among these we may mention ruled pads, composition books, boxed stationery and graph paper. The company was old and famous in its field, but over the years it had lost ground to the competition. The first of two major reasons for the loss was that many of the firm's products were out of date; there had been too little redesign and too few new items added. The second was that, like its products, the company's salesmen were old and reliable, and each year they got one year older and one year more reliable.

As the company slipped, Oliver advanced. In 1952, when sales had gone down to less than half of what they had been in 1939, his father-in-law retired and he became president. Oliver worked feverishly to save the company from disaster. He revamped some old items, dropped others, added new lines.

A study Oliver made of the sales force showed that in 1939

there had been sixteen salesmen calling on retail accounts; the youngest salesman was then thirty-five, the average age forty-six. Down to 1952 not one new man had been added. The sixteen had shrunk to twelve, four having quit. Now the average age was fifty-eight; the youngest man was fifty and the oldest seventy-four. Four others were sixty-five or over. Every man had been with the firm for at least two decades.

Oliver's problem with his salesmen would have been simpler if the company had had a retirement plan, but it had none, and he could not bring himself to fire loyal, long-time employees who were too old to find other employment. His solution, an expensive one, was a retirement plan that assured each man of a company pension of $3,000 per annum for life. Nobody would be obliged to retire for the next two years; thereafter each man over sixty would be subject to an annual review. If in Oliver's judgment the review showed a man was no longer carrying his weight, such employee would be given six months' notice of retirement. A salesman sixty-five or over could choose to retire at any time, without regard to the reviews.

Oliver presented his plan at a meeting of the salesmen. He explained the crisis the company was in, and the reasons for it. Then he told them he planned to build the sales force up to twenty as quickly as possible. The men took the news well, partly because they understood the problems, and partly because the retirement plan was so well worked out. Two announced their decisions to retire as soon as convenient.

The expenses of the retirement plan and the other innovations could not be met out of operating funds. To raise the money without going into debt, Oliver arranged to sell the firm's valuable building to an insurance company and then lease it back with an option to repurchase.

It took two years for all the brave new actions to produce results. Then, in 1955, sales were up by a meager 4 per cent; the next year they were up 12 per cent. In 1959, sales volume caught up with 1939; since then it has risen 10 per cent yearly.

In 1963, furthermore, Oliver bought out a competitor with an established position in the field.

It took new blood, Oliver's blood, to take the firm off the road to oblivion and put it back on the highway to the twenty-first century. But Oliver enjoys his work, and it's a good thing for him he does, because his door-to-door time away from home, on the job, averages seventy hours a week. To squeeze in that many hours, Oliver often works Saturdays; occasionally he's on the job Sunday, too.

But while he likes his work, Oliver gets less pleasure out of it each year. And when he has a day off, such as a Saturday or a Sunday, Oliver is "beat," as the children put it. He is so impressed by the importance of resting that he avoids almost every kind of activity except the most routine exercises, consisting of a few casual knee-bends before an open window. He often has headaches on his days off. Then he takes some aspirin and lies around the house looking frail, pale and useless.

There is not much wrong with this picture that a little bit of Oliver's good management cannot cure. Business is often like foreign affairs: Today's problem is tomorrow's history, and he who works on yesterday's problem today will be buried by tomorrow's new developments.

Oliver's problem has changed. In 1952 he had to save a valuable business from extinction. That challenge was worth almost any effort, and Oliver bent every fiber in his body to the task. By 1959 it was obvious that he had won the battle; advances since then have mostly been made by formula, even though human sweat is one of the ingredients. The problem years ago was survival; today it is continuity and growth. These are different propositions.

There are two reasons to urge that Oliver had better start having some fun outside his business. The first doesn't have much to do with our subject. It is that he will be more valuable to his firm, now and in the future, if he will start withdrawing from it, little by little. Why? Because, in order to withdraw at all, he will have to delegate some responsibility; thereby he will add to the firm's internal strength. Because a little withdrawal will give him a better perspective on company affairs; this will help him to evaluate his own work and the direction the business is taking. Because shorter hours will be fresher hours; he will be more effective on the job. Lastly, because he will live longer, and will therefore be able to serve the company over a greater span of years.

The second reason to urge Oliver to start having fun is that he has somehow got himself on a course leading straight to martyrdom, and he should get off that course now, though the effort be great. So far, Oliver has had a great success in life; he *is* a success. But the very things that have made him a success will make him a failure if he doesn't stop trying to solve last year's problem this year. That problem is licked; now the great challenge to Oliver, if he only knew it, is to arrange his affairs so that he can be as happy for the next thirty years as he has been for the last ten.

What makes Oliver run? Is he so poor that he has to work long hours, in order to collect overtime? No, it can't be that; his take-home pay and dividends add up to $50,000. Is he afraid he may be fired? No, again, because he has absolute control of the company. Is he fearful he may not have accumulated enough savings against his old age? Not likely; his worth outside the company is $200,000. Without figuring on the income potential of his stock in the company, he is already assured of a retirement income of $13,000, and it will likely go much higher.

No, Oliver is not running for any of these reasons. He is running partly out of habit and partly because he has set his business up so that it is wholly dependent on him. That's the way he wanted it, and that's the way he has got it.

He is slaving the way he is because he is playing God, and he doesn't know any better; but not knowing better need not mean he cannot learn. What he needs now, above everything, is a little philosophy. Here a horrible thought dawns: Wouldn't a mild heart attack be the best thing in the world for Oliver? It would force him to lie still for a few weeks; it would make him listen to his doctor; it would even make him think about his new situation. Perhaps, if this happened, he would go back to his job with a simple resolve that he *should* be able to arrive at without an attack, but may not—a resolve, that is, to teach his subordinates to run the business without checking every least decision with him. In fact, when he returned after his attack he might find things had run along smoothly enough without him. That should make him a happy and proud man.

If Oliver can perceive his new problem and whip it without first having a heart attack, so much the better. Delegate a little, then have a little fun; delegate a little more, have a little more fun—that might well be the pattern of his life for the next few years. He will almost certainly find that pattern if only he will seek it. Having discovered it, he will then begin to establish those other, larger patterns of enjoyment that will become increasingly important as he grows older. Whatever his choice of amusements, he will find, within broad limits, that the more fun he has, the more fun it is. He will live longer, and he will enjoy life the more.

The alternative may be to keep going along as he is until one day somebody or something pulls the switch on him. Then his friends, if any, can cluck their tongues and pontificate that there are some people who never learn.

So what'll it be, Oliver—tiddlywinks, ping-pong, bowling, a few hands of poker with beer on the side, some good books, or a course in classical Chinese literature? Or you name it.

Another man who is having no fun, but should be, is Vernon Hardy, manager of one unit in a chain of shoe stores. Vernon is the perfect example of the man who says, "Why pick on me?" when somebody suggests having a bit of sport. It's not just that he's the gloomy sort, you see, but that life is so tough for him. He is fifty-four now, and making about $9,000, which is quite a few bucks less than Oliver Oakley takes in. Still, nine grand is not starvation wages; ask the man who makes eight. Vernon feels secure in his job, and he is healthy. So what's the trouble?

The trouble is that Vernon is carrying a load that would throw a scare into a bull elephant. While Oliver has two grown-up children, both partly dependent, friend Vernon has four children, ages five through fourteen, all dependent now and for some years to come. He married late, but wasn't going to miss out on having some progeny because of that. And, believe it or not, old Vernon is also supporting his father, aged seventy-six, and Veronica Hardy's Grandma Gultch, age eighty-nine. Who else in the class is presently the sole support of a grandmother-in-law? Raise your hand, please.

This isn't the place to chat about Vernon's plans for retirement; our present subject is fun—remember? But I confess that when you think about Vernon's problems it does get a little hard to keep the subject firmly in mind.

Consider the pressures. Including himself, Vernon is supporting eight people, all living in his home. With so many dependents to feed, Veronica cannot contribute money to the household; she has to spend all her waking hours caring for her children and the old folks. Sometimes Vernon tries to think about saving money for his old age, but he is always reduced to shrugging off such frivolity. Anyway, he'll have his Social Security and a company pension of about $1,000.

Given that Vernon is stuck with eight bodies to clothe and shelter, eight mouths to feed, and sixteen feet to shoe, there can be little criticism of his slowness to put aside part of today's harvest for the golden years that lie up ahead. Like it or not, Vernon has to live in the here and now; he'll just have to take the sweet dalliance of the seventies when it comes.

But it is one thing for Vernon not to save for the future, and quite another for him not to have any fun. Somewhere he seems to have picked up the odd notion that fun and trouble don't mix, and it's exactly here that he is wrong. To keep his tensions under control, or, as Satchel Paige would put it, to keep his juices flowing, Vernon needs nothing so much as fun. If possible—but it's probably too much to expect—Vernon should try to have a little fun every day. The absolute minimum should be three times a week, and I do not refer here to his sex life. Depending on his tastes, he might spend one evening playing poker, another bowling or shooting pool with one of his sons, and a third out with Veronica. On weekends he might try going on picnics and hikes, playing ball with the kids, or perhaps casting a fishing line into a nearby lake or stream.

Note that some of these activities cost money, and that money is what Vernon has least of. So what? You only live once. And so long as you can enjoy life, the longer you do so the better. I guarantee Vernon will live longer and more happily if he will give up the pathetic notion that fun is not for him, and gets down to the serious business of having himself a good time. Does the fun money have to come out of the food budget? As I said before, so what? With so many people eating in the Hardy household, just the least bit less food for each person each day would provide all the fun money needed.

I'm serious about this. Nothing is more important than getting some pleasure out of life. Fun is certainly worth the money it costs when so little added expense can not only make the days bearable or even pleasurable, but may even prolong life—and will certainly improve it.

Ask Dr. Pitkin.

How Old Are You?

MUCH OF WHAT PEOPLE SAY to one another goes in one ear and out the other, and it's often just as well that way. Otherwise we might get the idea our acquaintances are fools, liars, and worse. Consider the following: On a scorching day two friends meet on a dusty plain to watch the approach of a tornado. "Good morning," says the first. "How are you?" His friend coughs noisily, tries to rub the grit from his eyes, then sneezes repeatedly. "I'm fine, thanks," he replies, intending no untruth.

A different illustration is the old saying, "You are only as old as you feel," a cheery and untrue statement long since worn smooth by overuse. Like "I'm fine," in the above example, it goes in one ear and right out again—just as it should.

Several years ago I saw a cartoon that showed a plump, female tourist talking to a Navaho in the American Southwest. "Tell me," said the woman, "how does it feel to be an Indian?"

Nobody knows how it feels to be what he is; the Indian is an Indian, and the woman has European forebears. How they feel is a function of their health, their mood, the news, the weather, the local incidence of mosquitoes, and so forth. It has nothing to do with their race, their nationality or their religion.

People do not feel old, although they often say they do. What they feel is tired; or they feel pain or boredom or discouragement, or some other dreary sensation or nonsensation which they associate with age. People *say* they feel old when they are discouraged. They blame age when their trouble is that they lack heart or courage. They have found a scapegoat, and they mean to use it.

In varying degrees the supposed symptoms of age affect the young as well as the old. When my mother was past sixty, she was bothered by arthritis in her fingers, and a cheerful aunt of ninety is nearly crippled by it. But then, too, I know an attractive young woman in her twenties who is plagued by arthritis. Does she say, "I feel old"? Not at all, because to her that would be ridiculous. What she says is, "Pass the aspirin."

Consider boredom. This today is even more a disease of youth than of age. Some of the young men with unkempt beards have a vast capacity for ennui; and for every bored young man with a beard there must be a thousand others, also asleep on their feet, who shave regularly. Yet people from forty to eighty persist in thinking that the boredom *they* feel is due to their age. This is nonsense. With them as with the young, protracted boredom is a sign of failure to face a problem or to accept a challenge.

We could, if we wished, examine most or all of the subjective symptoms of age cited by persons who claim to feel old; and in each case we would find that the identical symptom is known to multitudes of people of twenty and thirty, and probably to ten-year-olds, too. This would even hold for subjective symptoms of serious disease. So we who are over fifty really have no monopoly on any particular sensations, even though many of us find it convenient to believe the contrary.

This is not to say that there are no objective signs of aging. Dr. Edward J. Stieglitz points out in his book *The Second Forty Years,* that aging starts before birth and continues until the point of death, after which, he says, there is no more aging. So it seems prudent to agree with Stieglitz that people who grow older every day are luckier than those who do not.

The senses of taste and smell commonly decline with the years beyond early adulthood. And in greatly varying degrees, in different individuals, hearing and sight also become less acute. Such changes do not make us feel old, but they may lead us to wear our glasses, to turn up the volume on the phonograph, or to put a bit more spice on our meat.

Aging brings with it not only a toning down of the senses; it also brings a decline of the physical capacities. The boxer at age thirty-five is not, as a rule, a match for the twenty-four-year-old; forty is typically no match for thirty; sixty cannot generally expect to outpoint fifty. Strength, speed of reflex, and endurance all decline with the years past the early twenties.

But this is not all. To do our work and to lead healthy lives most of us who are past fifty require less food. And, while we should not go as long without sleep as younger persons may, it is often true that we need less sleep than our juniors do. Older people may be better off when they can work in a little nap during the day, or perhaps just before dinner.

Please observe how frequently I have used cautious, qualifying words and phrases such as "often," "in varying degrees," "some," "as a rule," "typically," and so forth. Why? Merely because people are always refusing to fit in with all the lovely generalizations that can be proved out only by studying thousands of cases. The fact that the social scientists have had to do just that does not make the generalizations more impressive; it makes them less so. For nobody is average, and any healthy fifty-year-old reader of these pages may need more sleep and more food than he did twenty years ago; he may be a better pugilist than most men of forty. But I do not recommend pugilism to anybody of either age.

The anatomical signs of aging include a decrease in the size and number of functioning cells in the vital organs and tissues and a resulting contraction in the size of the organs and of the entire organism. There is an increase in the amount of normal but nonfunctioning intercellular and connective tissues. The walls of the blood vessels tend to become thicker and less elastic, with the result that the vessels become less efficient. Among the results of this loss of efficiency are a falling off in the utilization of oxygen and a consequent reduction of function. There is a decrease in endocrine activity.

A summary report issued in 1953 also makes these points:

1. Strength of muscles declines with age, one investigation having shown that the strength of back muscles falls off by 18 per cent between age twenty-seven and age fifty. But the strength of arm and hand muscles declines less rapidly.

2. More striking than the reduction of muscle strength with age is a lessened ability for sustained hard work. Older people work nearer to their limits than younger people, and have smaller reserves to call upon in emergencies.

3. Ability to learn new material and memory of things recently experienced show a general decline with age. But judgment and the creative imagination reach their peak late and decline slowly if at all.

Over and over again, studies of aging come back to the following three themes:

1. The physical symptoms of aging are less open to dispute than mental changes, which may also be fairly clear. Tests to measure the effects of age on mentality are, to date, all more or less unsatisfactory.

2. Decreases in mental ability are greatest among those in dull, routine work and among others whose minds have not frequently been challenged over the years. As a rule, too, the abler the mind, the more slowly it ages. One study even indicated that, among

the brightest 5 per cent of the population, mental decline with age was very slight or even absent. A company making precision instruments has found that older men can learn a new job quickly when instruction and incentive are both good. Two weeks is enough time for these workers to master virtually any job in the plant. A fifth of this company's employees were over sixty when the study was made, and over a tenth were beyond seventy.

3. Each individual tends to age in his own individual way, which may be *different* from the way his brothers and sisters age and also *slower or faster* than the average rate of aging.

Physicians are agreed that there is typically a difference, and sometimes a wide difference, between a person's biological age and his age as measured in years. Someone who, by the calendar, is figured to be fifty years old, may closely resemble the average person of forty summers or be more like your aunt's idea of a sixty-year-old. And an even closer resemblance to thirty-five or sixty-five is not out of the question. So, looking at the extreme cases, we can say that in their physical get-up, in their work habits, in their habits of play, in their mental acuity, in their appearance, in their fund of energy, in their outlook on life, and in the sharpness of their senses, *two people of fifty may be as unlike each other, as if they were of different generations.* No wonder some people at the half-century mark can see the promise of great adventure where others behold only a wet dishrag!

For an illustration of this principle, let us look at the age indications of three octogenarians. At eighty years, Doe has impaired hearing and stiff joints; but he also has a magnificent circulatory system, fair eyesight, and impressive mental agility. Smith, the second octogenarian, is able to walk for miles without tiring and can recite countless tales from his childhood; but Smith's speech is slurred, he is unable to recall what he had for lunch ten minutes ago, and he does not know who is President of the United States. O'Leary, the third man, has a badly damaged circulatory system, an unreliable digestive tract, and kidneys that are only marginally adequate; but he has a bright, inquisitive mind, a good sense of humor, and surprisingly superior manual dexterity. All these men are eighty years old by the calendar. But how old is each man really—that is, biologically?

Except in clinically obvious cases—and most cases are not *that* obvious—it may be difficult to come to grips with the question, How old am I? The person of fifty, more or less, who wonders where he stands in life cannot be asking himself how old he is in calendar years; he knows that, anyway. Nor should he be asking the number of calendar years of life that remain to him; only God knows that, and He won't tell. What he might properly want, however, is a guide to his capacity for daily living, because such a guide can help him plan for the years and decades ahead. A perceptive doctor who has given a physical examination can come as close to the answer as anybody is likely to do, and he *should* report any obvious signs of ill-health or aging. Sometimes, though, key facts get lost behind an overdone bedside manner.

Still, it is hard for a doctor to know all the facts, and some of the negative but perhaps important impressions we make on others (rather like the fact of halitosis in the ads of years ago—"Even your best friend won't tell you") are unlikely to be reported in full candor. So, sooner or later each of us will have to work out the answer for himself. But good medical advice is essential in any case.

This is all very well and good! But, given all the necessary information, *what, precisely, is the formula for telling a man's or a woman's real age,* rather than merely his or her calendar age? Alas, there is no precise formula. Most certainly, there is no *concise* formula. If there were, I suppose I would not have written this book; and if I had, you would not be reading it.

Nevertheless, there is a kind of answer. So far as family and friends are concerned a person is as old as his view of life; a physical examination merely adds an essential other dimension to the answer. Looking at our three octogenarians in the light of such an analysis, we can say that Doe is a hobbled, youthful person (in balance, we could say he is in late middle age); Smith is a very old man; while O'Leary is, above all, an ailing man. If his mind were not so bright, we could call O'Leary a sick old man; but whenever we talk with him he makes us forget his age, and we think of him as one of us. He is plenty sick; but, as we say, "he's O.K."—that is, he is sharp, human, warm. We cannot think of him as old; only as frail.

It makes a difference whether a person's view of life includes himself as a doer or as an evaluator or as a mere bystander. One man I know has at fifty-five seen life as a procession in costume, passing him by. Because the costumes are often outlandish, to his eyes, he has become a scoffer. To a degree, this scoffing has preserved his role in the world and has kept him younger-seeming than a more passive but bitter woman, born at about the same time, who sees the world as an endless, uncrossable wall, on the other side of which important deeds are accomplished by daylight and where, in the dark of night, people engage in mysterious amusements. Without understanding anything, she hates modern life and feels she is 'out of it all.'

At any age beyond fifty we are apt to consider those people youngest who are most involved, physically and psychologically, in making a living, improving their homes, being artistically or otherwise creative, or doing volunteer community or organization work. Probably we should consider young in spirit, too, most of those who do a good amount of reading, whether for information, for amusement or for insight. The more selective the reading is, the more it tells about the person doing it. But the reading of nothing but trivia, whether in books or in magazines, may reflect laziness or an evasion of responsibility.

Not long ago a great doer, and a man younger than his years, was heralded in *The New York Times* under the headline, "Rodgers, at 60, Acts Younger Than Springtime." The article dealt with the activities of Richard Rodgers, the composer of music and author of Broadway shows. Rodgers, it seems, was an almost incredibly busy man at the time of his sixtieth birthday. He was writing a new show, he was attending rehearsals for replacements in the Broadway and national companies of *The Sound of Music,* and was otherwise employed. The story continues:

Almost daily, Mr. Rodgers is asked if a particular performer would be acceptable to him in a revival of a Rodgers and Hammerstein show.

"Tonight," he said, "there will probably be at least fifty productions of *Oklahoma!* Add to that *Carousel, The King and I, South Pacific, Allegro, Flower Drum Song.* I have three men working eight hours a day sending out the parts for the various productions."

Furthermore, there are fan mail and the many luncheons with friends who have a son or a nephew or a daughter who want to get into show business.

Then there are other activities. Mr. Rodgers is a director of the New York Philharmonic, the Juilliard School of Music and the American Society of Composers, Authors and Publishers. He is a trustee of Barnard College and a member of the advisory committee of the National Cultural Center and the council of the Dramatists Guild.

"The only days I accomplish any work writing songs are the days when I go to the country on week-ends," he said.

If Mr. Rodgers is working hard, he still finds it "exciting and fun." The future? "I would just like to have as much contact with as many people as I can. I'm very fortunate in working in a medium that makes it possible."*

We get another slant on aging when we say the odds are that what a person sees in the world is very much like what the world sees in him. A man may see the world as an exciting, colorful and delightful place. If so, the people in his world probably regard him as a bright and lively person. To another man life may seem like nothing so much as a humdrum movie he has sat through a hundred times before. He, in turn, will seem a boring, unimaginative or sour fellow.

It is a truism that we color the world with the glasses we choose to wear. "Oh, look out the window," says one female, laughing with delight. "It's snowing. Oh, isn't it beautiful?"

Her friend noticed the snow a minute ago, but said nothing. "Beautiful-schmeautiful," she now replies, puckering her face. "Snow melts and makes mud. Where are my rubbers?"

Two different outlooks, two different-looking women looking out the window!

It has often been remarked, by doctors and laymen alike, that people who have a strong will to live can be amazingly durable, while those who have lost the will to live are not long for this world. Now a strong will to live suggests a strong interest in life—that is, an interest in the day-to-day life of one's own world and not just a blind craving for survival. Throughout life we can observe that those who take a lively interest in things of this world seem younger than others of their years.

This raises a fascinating question. Can we *will* interest, that is, can we force ourselves to be interested in a good slice of life; and, having succeeded in this, do we then become younger than before, relative to our calendar age? Can Ponce de Leon's Fountain of Youth be turned on, like a faucet, by a mere act of will?

But isn't a decline of interest simply a function of biological decline and therefore, like the hand of God, beyond our control?

We must digress, and then we must digress from our digression, before we can properly come to grips with this important question; in the end, anyway, the answer must be each man's and each woman's own.

We know that if our heredity is good, we will be most likely to age slowly and live long, and it has been said that the first thing to do, if you want to live to a very old age, is to choose parents and grandparents who outlived the three score and ten years cited in the Bible. Studies of healthy centenarians show that an amazingly high proportion of their known forebears lived into their eighties. It is also surprising to find how many healthy persons of a hundred years and more live within a few miles of where they were born, how many are financially secure (but not wealthy), and how many show a cheerful interest in today and tomorrow.

Poverty, malnutrition, illness, or loneliness may speed up the aging process; poor physical environment may do it; overwork or physical strain may do so. Bad habits of eating, drinking, playing, working and loafing can have similar effects; so can excessive worry or discouragement. A loss of direction and a sense of discouragement following forced, unplanned-for retirement are often mentioned as the causes of the rapid aging that sometimes turns a youthful man of sixty-five into an old-timer of sixty-seven.

At fifty it is too late to choose our grandparents and too late to overcome the effects of malnutrition in childhood. But if we act now, it may be in time to avoid many of the ill effects of excessive eating, drinking, loafing, smoking, loneliness, or going to seed. A family physician can give sound advice on many such matters. Many physicians can also advise about retirement. Indeed, we should ask everybody we can to help shed light on this knotty problem, and we must think about it long and hard and—if we are the type—even prayerfully. For retirement is a potent circumstance of life that can break us—or make us.

Pension plans are extremely various, though many outmoded plans still set a fixed retirement age—often sixty-five. For each breadwinner fortunate enough to come under a pension and who can himself decide when to retire, or who can even share significantly in the decision, there are others who still have little choice in the matter.

One advantage of a fixed retirement age is obvious. A plan involving a flexible retirement age, depending on job output, may be difficult to administer, while a fixed age is easily dealt with. A specified retirement age shields the boss from the entreaties of long-time employees who feel they can still give years of valuable service to the company. It shields him, too, from department heads who want to keep a valuable man on the job after sixty-five. With a fixed age, *nobody* need shoulder the burden of decision. One man may be nearly worthless at fifty-seven, but since he is a long-time employee he will be kept on for eight years of further declining productivity, until he reaches the standard sixty-five-year retirement age. Another man is good for ten more years at the old job and is going to be very hard to replace. But he has already hit sixty-five, and is therefore retired forthwith.

Employers hire people only for their *individual* capabilities; but many employers retire employees only on the ground of their *average* limitations. Is your physiopsychological age fifty, and is your chronological age sixty-five? You must be retired *now,* lest the sacred routine be disturbed. The fixed-age formula may be grossly wasteful but, by heaven, it is simple!

The Meaning of Work and Retirement is the title of a wonderful book on the experiences and the beliefs of people from fifty-five to over eighty years of age. To gather information for the book, trained interviewers were sent out to talk with coal miners, steelworkers, salespeople, skilled craftsmen, and physicians. One of the threads the researchers turned up again and again was the opinion that retirement is no picnic and that a man who wants to be happy must keep on working. Here, for illustration, is part of an interview with a steelworker, age sixty-four:*

Q. Do you think you'll retire when you reach sixty-five?

A. No, not if I can get the doctor to say I'm okay to go back to work. They have a plan now that you don't have to retire.

Q. At what age should a man retire?

A. I don't think they should have to retire. If a man is alive at seventy, he can still work. When a man's used to exercise and work, he can't just quit and do nothing. The only way to stay alive is to keep working.

Now read the testimony of H., a sixty-five-year-old man, who, after a few years of retirement on his doctor's orders, went back to his work as a salesman in a high-class Chicago department store:

MR. H. I have no desire to quit. I feel that people are much better off if they are working, because their mind is better employed at something that you can get some kind of satisfaction out of. It isn't necessarily the money that makes me work. I got a lot ahead and could loaf for quite a while and wouldn't miss any meals at all.

Q. What did you miss most when you weren't working?

A. Well, I wasn't satisfied. I couldn't stay put any place. I used to come over to Chicago and spend a few weeks—my daughter lived here at the time—and then I'd go back to _____ that's where my home is, and I'd go down to Florida and spend maybe two or three months down there. And then down to

---

* Excerpts are from *The Meaning of Work and Retirement*, by Eugene A. Friedmann, Robert J. Havighurst, et al. Published by The University of Chicago Press. Copyright © 1954 by The University of Chicago. Reprinted by permission.

———. That was my old home and from there to ———, but I wasn't satisfied any place. So in order to get away from the monotony of loafing, when the job was offered to me, I took it. I have no intention of quitting. If they want to kick me out, they kick me out. Well and good.

Q. Do you think at any time that you will? Maybe not in the natural set of years, but do you think of any time that you might change or that you would want to quit?

A. No, I don't. I was so sick of trying to retire . . . that I think that, as long as I'm able to get around on my job, I'm going to be on the job. When I get to a point where I'm not able to carry out my end of it, I hope the Lord takes me off this earth so I won't be a bother to somebody else.

The same book reports a survey among 138 doctors age sixty-five and over. All had private practices and were therefore free to keep on working as long as they wished, or until ill-health forced them to retire; they could also quit whenever they wanted to. Ninety-three of the doctors were still working full time or part time, but almost all who were still active had cut back on their work in one way or another. Some said they had eliminated night visits, some had cut out all home calls, others had given up surgery. The amount of work done varied with the age, but some were still actively practicing past the age of seventy-five. With nearly complete freedom of choice, these men carry on. Why? The reasons vary, but Dr. J. seems to have spoken for a number of these physicians.

He stated that he enjoyed doing some work even if he could not work full time. He went on to say that he felt that the trouble with some people is that they give work a negative connotation. They talk about play as though it were something positive, and about work as something negative. Dr. J. felt that people should realize that work meant "fulfillment of self." He pointed out that only through work could a person find coordination of mind and body.

No doubt work does mean "fulfillment of self" to many people. And to these and others it is also an absorbing way to pass the time.

Now meet Dr. S., a widower who makes his home now with his son and daughter-in-law and their children. Dr. S. maintains a nine-to-five working schedule and limits all his work to his office. He breaks up this routine by lengthy yearly vacations. Dr. S. does not believe that this harms his practice, since he always has an office full of patients waiting for him the day he comes back from one of his trips.

When asked why he continued working, Dr. S. said, "I have enough money to retire, but I don't know what I would do. There are only two things that I know, and these are farming and medicine. I have been practicing medicine so long that I don't think I would like farming again."

And so we see that many (but not all) of those whose opinions are set down in *The Meaning of Work and Retirement* found positive values in their work and were reluctant to retire. A question that came up again and again was, What would I ever do with myself if I were to retire? But a minority looked forward with pleasure to retirement.

Millions of intelligent men and women work at dull jobs, and the tendency is always for work to become more routinized and therefore duller and duller. Such employment offers no challenge to the old hand. Yet the job gives him a role in life, and the pay is good for meeting the mortgage and insurance payments.

Possibly the worst thing about the dull job is that those who work at it sometimes make themselves over in its image by routinizing their free time as much as their bosses have routinized the work. It is not just that the work day has been laid out with fixed hours of rising, eating, going to work, returning from work, and retiring; that is bad enough. What is worse is that the routine worker may become a routine liver, even down to the smallest details of his off-time rest and play. He may also become a routine thinker—or nonthinker, most often, because that is easier.

If the nonthinking, overroutinized worker does not seem older than his years that may be because his moment of truth is not yet, but later, when he retires. Then he will find that his domestic timetable, so carefully chiseled out to meet the demands of his job, is wholly inadequate to the pressing demands of his new freedom. If he would think ahead, he could now avert a situation in which his days will be given over to fretting, his nights to tossing and turning as he tries to decide what to do with himself. Because he does not think much about anything—even though he is inherently intelligent—he is most likely to become one of those unlucky fellows for whom retirement is really not much fun.

It is important for those in routine jobs to start building outside interests at about fifty. We are not all doctors, and we cannot all be Richard Rodgers, who finds all the human contacts and stimulation he needs right on the job, and who, being self-employed, will not retire until he is good and ready. When boredom sets in, if that is conceivable, Rodgers can run up to the country and write a song; it's all in a day's work. The non-self-employed owe it to themselves to develop off-job activities that will engage their minds and their imaginations as thoroughly as his work engages Rodgers.

If the person with a routine job is at one hazardous extreme, the man or woman with a fascinating occupation may be at the other, somewhat less hazardous extreme. The marvel of the most interesting jobs is that they absorb our creative energies and attention without dulling us. Because such jobs keep us in touch with things outside ourselves and with other people, they also help us keep a young outlook; again, witness Richard Rodgers. The danger is that we may be so absorbed in our work that we never quite see what we are becoming; and we are all becoming older, both by the calendar and in our body cells. For many, aging by the calendar may be the more dangerous, because at about sixty-five many whose work is so wonderful are going to be retired, ready or not. The chances that a person in such a job will be ready to retire are only middling; the work may be so absorbing that he too will have neglected to build up any outside interests.

It is a good thing that so many occupations lie between the extremes of dull routine and constant challenge. The great majority of employees in the middle-of-the-road jobs find worktime satisfactions that add to the money value of the job. Neither overly absorbed nor utterly bored, these people are most apt to prepare wisely and well against the day of their retirement.

Who are in this middle group?

There is the secretary to the president of a small company. After ten years on the job she finds her work mostly dull, but once in a while she has an interesting problem to cope with. Luckily, she likes her boss and some of the other secretaries. About once a month she does a little sly drinking at lunch with friends. During the daily coffee break there is kidding around, and she enjoys the two office parties that are held each year. Small satisfactions, but genuine nevertheless.

Then there is the boss. He is not the sole owner of the business; it is a family affair. The possibilities for expansion seem limited, and he sometimes finds it necessary to work long hours just to keep things going. He has a fair sense of humor, he is not under the thumb of a remote stockholder group working through a cold-blooded board of directors, and he feels the company performs a valuable service.

The owner of a garage and service station has the usual satisfactions of the owner and operator of a business. Almost every motion of himself and his employees has significance to him, in relation to his goals of profit and growth. He likes to be of service to his customers, he likes to plan improvements, he enjoys a little horseplay with the help, even though he pays for time so spent. But, like most bosses, he works long hours; he has trouble finding and keeping good help; he often feels he does not earn enough money for his effort.

A man who has spent his working life with the government, with an insurance company or a bank, or in the office of a large corporation, in a nonselling position, below the level of senior executive, may feel that life has become dreary. A dulling monotony of work, of hours, of prospects, of pay, and of associations may pall on him. But there are compensations, including job security, friendships with a few associates, often a sense of the social value of the work being done, a belief that one's own contribution is outstanding, and pride of identification with the organization.

Secretaries, engineers, foremen, executives, teachers, salesmen—all these groups, and many others, contain large numbers of people who, at fifty, are neither bored stiff nor thrilled beyond words. Mostly, their jobs need not blind them to the distance from here to sixty-five.

They can easily take thought of the problems to come, and what should be done to meet them. They *can;* but not all of them do so.

Man often acts most wisely when he is afraid. A person who sees that the building he lives in has started to collapse gets out fast. But sometimes the wisdom that fear teaches comes too late. If the structure has not shown signs of weakness, and the tenant has nothing to go by but the routine warning of an engineer, he may decide to stay on for a while. Then, one day when he is napping, the building falls in on him.

Those who fail to plan ahead for retirement are a little like the sleepyhead who takes a snooze after the engineer has warned him to get moving. Fifty or fifty-five is not too late to feel a little afraid of what's in store—it's certainly not too early—but he who waits in apathy for enforced retirement may wake up on the appointed day to find it is too late to plan a party for that evening.

Much of life is getting ready. Kindergarten gets the tot ready for first grade, first grade for second grade. High school is considered a necessary prelude to college. You cannot go to a graduate school in medicine, law, philosophy or government if you have not got your baccalaureate. To practice law, to teach philosophy or jurisprudence, one must have attended graduate school. A doctor must serve an internship at a recognized hospital before he can hang out his shingle. Young women, looking forward to marriage, store away linens and other household necessities in a hope chest, or, as they say in England, in the bottom drawer.

The age of fifty is not a moment too soon to start learning and getting ready for retirement. A good part of getting ready is mental exercise; much of the part that is not mental, but is active, is highly enjoyable. The girl's hope chest is not too bad a parallel; she may have nearly as much fun accumulating the linens as she does using them later. But not quite.

How old are you? Maybe younger than your years, by a long shot; but still old enough to start thinking about retirement!

P. G. Wodehouse
and Some Other Cutups

DID YOU EVER STOP to think that youth is largely a state of mind? Or that even young people tend to grow to the age of their mental processes? Nagging anxiety can overcome a chronic case of youth in just a few years; given the right attitude, the young man of twenty-five readily becomes the old fussbudget of thirty.

Anxieties and loneliness can have a like effect on older people, a fact confirmed in a report issued in 1963 by a team of twenty-two scientists attached to the National Institute of Mental Health. A study of forty-seven reasonably healthy men between sixty-five and ninety-two convinced these learned men that the sixty-five-plus can stay remarkably young if they retain their health. But the study also showed that psychological responses to such things as the loss of friends "may amplify, if not initiate, changes in the older nervous system and thereby in the rest of the organism."

And so we see that age, if not simply a state of mind, is nevertheless shaped by one's outlook. This is true even of biological age, according to the scientists cited above. People are not as old as they feel, but they are as old as their thinking, or soon become so. Let things bother you, allow yourself the luxury of prolonged worry, and you grow old.

Victor Moore, the comedian who in 1932 played Vice-President Alexander Throttlebottom in George Gershwin's comedy *Of Thee I Sing,* knew something about life and laughter. Twenty years later, when he was seventy-six, Moore won wide acclaim for his starring role in the Broadway hit revival of *On Borrowed Time,* the Paul Osborn play. Then in show business for sixty years, he found it necessary to deny unfounded rumors that he was planning to retire.

He said he didn't think he was so old, and that he had aged more than seventy-six years betting on just one horse race when his bankroll was growing thin and the horses were dragging their hoofs. He couldn't imagine quitting work, he continued, because he was enjoying himself so much playing in *On Borrowed Time.* He said if he retired he would only go back to the race track, "and pretty soon I would have to go back to work again."

As we read about amusing people beyond the usual retirement age, we may well wonder whether there isn't something more to be said than "Laugh, and the world laughs with you." Indeed there is, and Victor Moore was not noted for his own laughter. Laughter has its own great therapeutic value, but it was work that kept Moore going; making others laugh was merely his line of work.

Keeping Victor Moore in mind, let us look in on some of the several hundred centenarians studied by Dr. Flanders Dunbar a few years ago. One of Dr. Dunbar's interviewers called on a Maine woman, age 109, who proudly showed him an apple orchard she owned. "When they returned to the house," Dr. Dunbar says, "the interviewer commented on the deliciousness of the apples. Whereupon she said, 'If you wait a minute I'll run out and pick some for you.' He said, 'No, let me do it when I get ready to go. I would rather talk with you.' She said, 'All right, I'll send the boy.' The boy who brought in the apples turned out to be her nephew, age ninety-nine."*

When I first came across this case I laughed out loud, and

* From a report delivered by Dr. Dunbar at the Third Congress of the International Association of Gerontology in London, 1954.

so did the people I mentioned it to. But as one man has wisely pointed out, the humor in the situation is wholly in our minds. There was nothing funny about it, and nothing bitter, either, to the lady or to the "boy," her nephew; they were far too busy living to waste time laughing over such trifles. They were simply active people who, like so many of the other centenarians in the study, lived in the present, attended to their business, and did not think it especially interesting that others got a kick out of their being so sprightly.

It has often been remarked that a surprising number of people beyond the century mark continue to be gainfully employed, generally in some independent or semi-independent line of work. Dr. Dunbar discovered a 100-year-old banker, who said he was hard on his shoes and whose favorite expression was, "A man on his feet is worth thirty on their seats." One lady who had worked all her life was busy making and selling needlework, in order to put her great-grandchildren through college. Many centenarians not gainfully employed were doing their own housekeeping. One woman of 113 had been persuaded to let others do her cleaning for her; then she caught the first cold she could remember having. Said she, "I just saved myself in time from dying by going back to doing my own housework."

Dr. Dunbar says, "Centenarians . . . are optimists according to the definition: 'An optimist is one who believes the future to be uncertain.'" They do not waste precious hours sitting in their rocking chairs, discussing the good old days, but show a lively interest in matters such as who will be the next President, what new things will be invented over the next few years, and so on. As a rule, they have many friends, and they know how to laugh.*

An echo of the story of the 113-year-old lady who went back to work for her health is heard in the case of young Charles Gibson, age eighty-five, who retired from farming a

* See Appendix for an account of some other centenarians.

few years back. Being a cardiac patient, he had been advised by his physician to take very light exercise; but the only exercise he got at first was in his rocking chair, where he sat and worried for two long months. Then somebody suggested he try playing pool, a game that would gently exercise his legs, arms and back. This was just what the doctor had ordered, so Mr. Gibson bought a pool table.

His first partner at pool was a little neighborhood girl. From her, and from others, he learned that many young children badly needed supervised recreation. This led him to set up the Gibson Home Recreation Club, a social and game center in his own home. Before long he was installing other games and amusements, and the center was a success. In the first summer of operation over a hundred children joined. During the school year the center was open to older people, but closed to children; then a few men came in each day to play pool.

In performing a community service, Mr. Gibson did himself a favor. Active public service gave him responsibility and an activity. It took his mind off his troubles.

A cornerstone of my father's philosophy of growing old and liking it was his belief that the person beyond forty should stay in what he called "the hot center of things." Over and over he said that the man or woman who has left his thirties behind should "keep moving," because activity, to Walter B. Pitkin, was living at its best.

What is the moral of all this? Is it "Work, and the world works with you; vegetate, and you go to seed"? When we work, not necessarily at a job somebody has given us, we are members of that good company of men and women who are busy providing for themselves, or who are bettering their community and the world, or who merely help others. Work gives us a sense of purpose, of our own dignity. Work puts us in touch with the future; being optimists, we think we may have a stake in that future. When we work, we have no time to be bothered by the problems of those who only vegetate, and on whom time weighs so heavily—as it weighed on Mr. Gibson before he got out of his rocking chair. Working, we have no time to reminisce, no time to fret, no time to worry, no time to take the mournful count of the days and years.

When he was eighty, the incomparable P. G. Wodehouse added another book to the seventy-odd novels and story collections he had published down to then. Called *Author! Author!,* it consists of letters he wrote to a close friend during the years 1920–1961. The following excerpt is from the last letter in the book, written after Wodehouse had reviewed the earlier correspondence:*

It has to be faced. I'm slowing up. I still do my before-breakfast exercises every morning, plus touching my toes fifty times without a suspicion of bending the knees, and I can navigate my daily three miles, but I can see I'm not quite the man I was.

Little changes tell the story. . . . I am noticeably less nimble when getting after the dog next door if I see him with his head and shoulders in our garbage can. And I note a certain stiffness of the limbs which causes me, when rising from my chair, to remind the beholder, if a man who has travelled in Equatorial Africa, of a hippopotamus heaving himself up from the mud of a riverbank. . . .

The hot blood of the late seventies has cooled. Today when I see a sexagenarian—Frank Sullivan, as it might be, or somebody like that—climbing a tree, I smile and say to myself, "Boys will be boys. When you are my age, child," I say to myself, "you will realize that the true pleasures are mental."

I am eighty and may quite easily go to par, and I find I am quite happy just sitting and thinking, or at any rate sitting. I can detach myself from the world. And if there is a better world to detach oneself from than the one functioning as of even date, I have yet to hear of it.

The great thing about being an octogenarian is that you can legitimately become set in your ways. I have always wanted to do this, but in the old days something was always happening to prevent it. . . . Today in my quiet rural retreat I do the same things day after day, with no variation. Morning exercises, breakfast, work till noon, watch *Love of Life* on television, lunch, take the dogs to the post office, walk back, more work, cocktails, dinner, and then the quiet evening with a Rex Stout or an Erle Stanley Gardner. Monotonous? Not a bit of it. I love it. The cry goes around Remsenburg, "Wodehouse has found his niche." And an octogenarian, mind you, is not expected to go to parties. The thought that I shall never have to wear a paper hat again is a very sustaining one. . . .

Another compensation for being a very old party is that by the time you reach eighty you have become more tolerant. Your kid of seventy-five is full of juvenile prejudices, but we octogenarians are able to take the broader, kindlier view. We accept someone like Fidel Castro or Nikita Khrushchev as part of the great plan, knowing that he must have been put into the world for some purpose, though with our finite minds we cannot understand what that purpose was. Perhaps we are not meant to understand.

So, on the whole, I have no objection to being eighty. Fortunately, perhaps, for there seems to be nothing I can do about it.

Note that with all the time out for quiet laughter, exercise, and reflection, Wodehouse, at eighty, was still hard at work.

Some Home Truths

"THERE'S A GREAT TIME COMIN', and it's not far off." So folk singer Burl Ives quotes Nicodemus the slave who, full of years and knowing he is near death, asks to be awakened on Judgment Day. The old slave, having lived righteously, eagerly looks forward to a time when the rewards will be passed out, as they never were in his lifetime.

What Nicodemus had, that many people today wish they had, was the magic quality of certainty. He was certain that he had lived a just life, certain that there would be a Judgment Day, certain he would be among those chosen to celebrate "the great Jubilee."

It was his life of toil, his carrying of his share of the burden, and more than his share, that gave him his sense of righteousness. Is it too much for us to assume that without his everlasting labors, thrust upon him by a hard master, Nicodemus might have become fretful and grown an ulcer in his middle age, and then died, not much later, halfway between doubt and fear?

The American slave was attached to an owner who intended his slaves to work long and hard to produce the maximum of wealth for the owner. While a slave might be temporarily excused from work because of illness, a stupid master might require him to work even when seriously ill. Certainly, he was expected to go on working for as many years as he was able; but old slaves were commonly given easier jobs than younger ones, not because the owners were soft-headed or paternal, but because it was plain good management to work the different slaves according to their differing abilities.

The Southern slaveholder, for practical and humanitarian reasons, was committed by law and by custom to support his aged slaves in idleness when they were no longer fit to work—though there was nobody to tell him when the time had come for a slave to be permanently retired from the fields. So, most slaves had little need to wonder what they would do in their old age; they knew they would go on working as long as they were able, and that they would go on being fed and sheltered until death overtook them. As awful and as inescapable as this knowledge may have been, how many Americans, North and South, are today without this certainty, and wish they had it—although not at the cost of being enslaved?

The lot of the typical Northern farmer of Nicodemus's time was infinitely better than that of the slave. His shelter was tighter, roomier, and cleaner; his clothing was superior; his food was better; and his freedom to improve his situation, as by moving elsewhere, was a great advantage. If he felt ill and in need of rest, he alone was the judge of when to stop working. He was a free man, and fiercely proud of his freedom. In some ways he was freer than most Americans of the nineteen sixties; but he had to toil long and hard to make ends meet. He knew full well that his lot was to work and then to die. Indeed, many farm men and women wound up doing both on the same day.

The aging Northerner who owned a farm before 1900 was usually the head of a farming family. The farm was worked by himself, his wife, usually one or more children, and possibly some grandchildren. One or more brothers or cousins may have helped on the same farm or operated an adjacent one. As the old man's physical capabilities declined, so did the difficulty of the work he had to do. Since there was always easy work as well as hard labor, the old fellow had to be pretty far gone to be without any useful function. If necessary, he could stop work altogether and let the others carry the full load. But if his health improved again, even after the age of eighty, you could pretty well count on seeing him back on the job and glad of it. After all, he reasoned, who wants to lie around the house all the time, being completely useless, when there is work to do? Like Nicodemus, the old-time Northern farmer had no nagging doubts about what he would do on reaching the age of sixty-five; he knew he would work and that he would wish he were a young man again.

Many a fifty-year-old can see his own situation in a new light by comparing it with that of the landed farmer of yesterday. To make this comparison easier, let us look in on one Meyer Mueller, born on May 1, 1780, on his father's place in a rich farming area in eastern Pennsylvania.

As a boy Meyer was somewhat frail, so that he was not much use around the farm before he was ten. (Karl, his strapping elder brother, had carried a heavy load of work from the age of eight.) From ten to twelve Meyer worked at the lighter chores. He cut kindling to length and carried the firewood, putting some by each fireplace; he carried the kitchen swill to the swine; he hauled the water from the well to the house. Later on he was given heavier work, and by the time he was fifteen he was laboring in the fields with the horses.

Free public education did not come to Pennsylvania until 1835, so it is not strange that Meyer never progressed far in book learning. But only two miles away there was a one-room Lutheran school which he walked to, off and on, from the age of seven until he was twelve. Here he learned some Bible lore, how to add, subtract and multiply, and how to read and write German legibly, with suitable decorative flourishes. Meyer had no occasion to learn English, and until he was thirty he knew nobody who spoke that strange tongue.

The old Mueller property covered 330 acres, of which 100 acres were pasture and orchard, 60 acres were in hay, 70 acres were tilled, and 100 acres were woodland. The pasture was used for grazing the work horses, a few calves, some milk cows, a bull and a few sheep. A corner of the pasture, adjoining the barnyard, was reserved for swine. The tilled land produced wheat and oats, which were the chief money crops; corn for the animals; and vegetables for the kitchen. The Muellers were especially proud of their orchard, which produced an abundance of delicious apples, peaches and cherries.

When Meyer was eighteen, Karl, two years older, had found himself a girl and announced that he wanted to marry. The father, Hans, then called a meeting of the Mueller men and Mrs. Mueller. The time had come, he said, to decide about the future. Karl was his eldest son, was his first descendant to be married, and would be the father of his first grandchildren. Clearly, Karl would inherit the farm; but that would happen later. Meanwhile, a two-room log cabin should be built for him. The time to do that was in the fall, after the harvest was in.

Hans Mueller pointed out that there were other things to be considered. Meyer was a man now, and he would want to get married too, pretty soon. And what was Meyer to do, share the farm with Karl later on, after Hans died? That would not be good, said Hans, because a brother does not make a good master, and there must always be a master. A place would have to be found for Meyer. Maybe Charlotte, Meyer's sixteen-year-old sister, could help. If she were married off to the Schroeder son, perhaps an arrangement could be made to get a corner of the big Schroeder place for Meyer. The Schroeders were not using all that land anyway, and only one son and one daughter had survived childhood. The Schroeder daughter did not look well; under no circumstances was Meyer to marry her. Better be a blacksmith or work for your brother than be a farmer with a sick woman always in the house.

Before long Charlotte Mueller did marry the Schroeder son. Now that the families were allied, Hans found it possible to bargain for some land for Meyer. Since the Schroeders were unwilling to part with more than forty acres, Hans decided that Meyer should also have forty acres from an adjoining part of the Mueller farm. Eighty acres would not be a big place, but the soil, all in timber now, was of the best. All in all, it should be enough to keep Meyer from moving away.

The price for the Schroeder land was high, but Hans paid it all out right away, in kind and in money. The eighty acres were then deeded to Meyer on the understanding that he would not improve them for at least five years. This was to give him time to work out repayment to his father.

Because he was a second son, without farmhouse or cleared land, it was hard for Meyer to marry well; but he married anyway, and got a few sticks of furniture, an old work horse and a calf for dowry. It was little better than nothing, but Meyer had no complaints. His woman, Hilda, was strong and willing, and there was lots of work to be done. Their first child, a boy, was born in the old Mueller house in August, 1805; early in October, Meyer built a cabin on his own land. He and Hilda moved into the cabin as soon as it was ready, and almost immediately he set to work clearing the land. His mother died in 1807.

At first Meyer kept his own family in victuals by working part-time for his father, but by 1810 he had a going farm that was self-sufficient. Then he built a proper house. In 1820 he was using all his land for crops and pasture, except for ten acres left in trees.

Early in the spring of 1821, when only one of the children was old enough to do heavy labor, Meyer came down with typhoid fever. His father, seeing that Meyer needed him more than Karl did, came over every day for a month to work at the plowing and seeding. In that year Hans was sixty-two and Meyer was forty-one.

A bit later the senior Schroeders came down with the same

ailment. For weeks the Mueller men helped out on their neighbors' place, while the women cared for the sick couple. Then Mr. Schroeder died; a day later his wife followed him.

Hans admired the way Meyer had built his farm up from nothing. Now he counseled his fully recuperated younger son to strike a bargain with his bereaved brother-in-law for more land, quickly, before the ten surviving Schroeder children, Hans's grandchildren by his daughter Charlotte, were big enough to be of use on the neighbors' big farm. Meyer agreed, and before long he had made a deal to take over forty acres of forest from the Schroeders in exchange for some money and three years' help with crops.

Of Hilda's nine children, five survived infancy. They were Heinrich, born in 1805; Wilhelmina, 1809; Georg, 1811; Ludwig, 1814; and Anna, 1816. Meyer counted himself fortunate that his whole family was healthy and that there was so much work to do; besides all the regular chores, there were now forty more acres to be cleared of trees.

The Napoleonic Wars had disrupted world trade in wheat, and for many years the Pennsylvania Dutch had profited mightily from inflated wartime prices. But now the wars were long over, and there was much grumbling over the low price of wheat. But having little land available for the crop, Meyer had almost no reason to complain. For him, at least, the years after 1827 were a time of growth and prosperity. From 1827, he and Hilda and all five children worked the land and improved the outbuildings. Their four regular sources of money income in those years were dairy products, fruit, oats and fattened animals. Each year the Meyer Muellers drove to market in Lancaster up to a dozen swine and half as many prime beef cattle.

In 1832 Meyer's father died in the same room and bed in which he had been born seventy-three years earlier, in 1759. In his later years Hans had earned his keep by working at such light jobs as repairing harness, painting, and tending the kitchen garden. But the work he liked best was cabinet making. For years he had been turning out more chairs, tables, dressers and other furniture than the Muellers and the Schroeders had any use for. The excess was sold in Lancaster.

Heinrich, Meyer's eldest son, had taken his bride with him, in 1827, to live with Hans in the old house. On the latter's death, Karl took over the old house and Heinrich moved back with his father; but by this time Wilhelmina and Georg had married and moved away. Anna followed. Since Heinrich would inherit Meyer's farm, this left only Ludwig to be provided for. The problem was taken out of Meyer's hands later on, when Ludwig was killed trying to stop a runaway horse.

Now both in their mid-fifties, Meyer and Hilda were feeling the results of most of a life spent at hard labor. Although strong and vigorous, they sometimes experienced aches for which there was no explanation except that they were getting on. But they could not let up, and did not want to. Where there had been seven people to do the work a short time earlier, there were now only four, including Heinrich's wife, who had young children to care for. They had decided, furthermore, to add two rooms onto the house to make it more agreeable for the three generations living there. And so for a few years more the grandparents went on working just about as hard as ever. The addition to the house pleased them, and they were glad that, with four workers instead of seven, the money income fell only a little.

By 1840, when Meyer was sixty, both he and Hilda had found it necessary to rest more and to cut down on heavy work, even at harvest. Most of the tasks in the barn and in the fields now had to be left to Heinrich and Lisa, his wife. Meyer and Hilda took charge of the four milk cows and ran the house and the kitchen garden. During rest periods, which became increasingly long for both of them, Hilda liked to do quilting and to make clothes for her grandchildren, while

Meyer busied himself with wood carving. As with his father before him, the odd jobs such as harness repairing, painting the barn, and so on, fell to him in his old age. As long as he was in tolerable health, which he usually was, he did his work well and slept soundly.

In 1843 Meyer found that he got weak spells if he did any hard work whatever, and so he had to give it up for good. Milking cows had become too difficult, and he would not trust himself on a ladder. Now he would paint only what he could reach from the ground, leaving the rest to others. At about this time, two of the grandchildren became old enough to be of help. So, although Meyer's strength was waning, affairs on the farm were again looking up.

By 1850, when he was seventy, Meyer had given up all farm work except a little light repairing. But he kept up his wood carving, turning out tableware, weather vanes and the inevitable American eagles. Meyer continued along these lines until 1856 when, after a short confining illness, he died. Hilda, who still seemed healthy, died a year later. It did not occur to anybody to feel guilty because at the age of seventy-five she was allowed to work in the kitchen or anywhere else she pleased. That was her business, as long as she felt she could do the work. And there were no better cooks than Hilda in the country between Reading and Lancaster.

For its time, the story of Meyer and Hilda is in no way re-markable. True, both lived longer than most people, but nobody is average, and many lived longer than the Muellers. While their Pennsylvania land was the richest in the nation, their neighbors had much more of it than Meyer had. And even though he was a fourth-generation American, Meyer still had to clear his own land, just as his emigrant great grand-father Mueller had done before him. The apparent good health which the family enjoyed was partly the result of natural selection. The weak died young.

Do the Muellers strike us today as an almost ideally happy

family? Their happiness is an illusion. It is a happiness which we project into an unfamiliar, long-ago situation. The Muellers were far too busy to be happy; they were too busy in their youth and too busy in their middle and old age.

This is not to say that they were incapable of moments of great pleasure, which might be called happiness. We might say that the Muellers were extremely happy right after their marriage, that Hilda was happy each time she gave birth to a live, healthy infant, and that Meyer was happy when he could at last move onto his own land, having waited so long. But if the Muellers were generally too busy to be happy, they were too busy to be unhappy. Of course, at moments of loss, as when there was a death in the family, they were exceedingly unhappy—or so we might say.

But "happiness" is a silly word to use in connection with the Muellers. It is much more fitting to say that they were *content* with their lives; for surely they were not discontented. The building up of a property, the hard work and the good food and the rural life among people of similar background and tastes agreed with them. Another thing that agreed with them was their security. And it is this, more than anything else, that attracts us to the Muellers' way of life. It is precisely the security of the old-time farmer that often leads modern city people to believe they too would like to farm.

Just how secure were the Muellers, anyway?

There is no measuring stick to help us answer that question. Some of their security was owing to the circumstance that no man had it in his power to tell Meyer what to do. The food the Muellers needed was taken from the soil by their own hands—all but the salt, the spices, the molasses, and a few other such things. Like other Eastern farmers of his time, Meyer had a paid-up reservoir of good will with his relatives and with unrelated people around the countryside. In a pinch, these relatives and neighbors could be relied upon to help him out; if the pinch was on his neighbors, he would help them. And it was probably not very embarrassing to ask for help—a little bit, but not much more so than applying for unemployment relief today.

To get the feel of the Mueller security, since we cannot measure it in dollars, let us guess what might have happened in case of disaster.

Suppose Meyer's sickness had crippled him for life.

For a few years the burden on Hilda would have been very great. Hans, who had been coming over to help, would not have been able to keep on doing as much heavy work as he did in the one month of Meyer's actual illness. The best that could have happened, then, is that Hans, Karl, and Karl's sons would have come over from time to time when the need was greatest. Meyer's own children would have been pressed into service a little earlier than they in fact were. Within five years, with the youngest child ten years old and Heinrich twenty-one, the farm would have been surging ahead anyway. And while the other children might have married and moved away, Heinrich, who would inherit the place, never would do so. So Meyer would have had shelter and food and care for the rest of his life—right in his own home.

Suppose the house had burned down, killing both parents when the children were young.

The children would have moved in with Karl and Hans. Later on, Heinrich would have inherited his father's farm, just as he did anyway.

Suppose Heinrich and his wife had decided to kick Meyer out when he reached sixty-five.

This is ridiculous. Until he was seventy, Meyer still carried his own weight, and even after that he was able to help out a little. Furthermore, it would never have occurred to Heinrich to be so cruel to his own father, who, in any case, still had title to the property. So if anybody went out into the cold, it would have been Heinrich, who owned nothing so long as his father was around.

The story of the hard-working Muellers shows how, in a simpler age, the roots people put down in their earlier years gave them a claim to this world's goods after the prime of life was gone. The system that protected the Muellers from want scarcely exists today; that is why we must have Social Security, pensions, unemployment insurance, hospital insurance and other social devices, to ward off life's harsher blows.

But the Muellers had one type of security which government has still not devised for today's landless millions. This was the security of their place in life; it meant not merely that they would be able to live out their days in their own home, but also that they were expected to work until they were no longer able.

Does this sound cruel? It is hard to believe it was. For without work, the old farms grew up in weeds and the people hungered. So the elderly farmer who helped keep things shipshape was an important person, quite aside from his position as head of family. And who does not like to feel needed, to feel important?

Today not one person in a hundred can come close to copying the Muellers' way of life. But reading their story and thinking about it may nevertheless shed useful light on our own, modern situation. Some, reading between the lines, may find a suggestion of the pleasures of a new occupation or other role in life, after the children are gone and when retirement is around the corner.

It's not a bad idea—as I say again and again in these pages.

Yesterday and Tomorrow, Wanting and Getting

MEN AND WOMEN of fifty who do not already do so should teach themselves to believe that the future belongs to them. It is well, too, to study the future as diligently as a good young student studies his history. Then, as the shape of the world as it will be ten, twenty and thirty years hence becomes less fuzzy in their minds, they should ask themselves whether they like what they see emerging. If so, they should work to bring that future about and to become a part of it. If not, they should strive to change the trend of things, so that their world of tomorrow may be more to their liking.

Ah, I am asked, but isn't history more fascinating than the future? Isn't what has already happened easier to know than the things we seek in a clouded crystal ball? At fifty and beyond, do not our true interests naturally lie in the past?

Lord knows, I am not one to close the door on history. I know of no pastime more enjoyable, and I am acquainted with no study that gives more insight into the world as it is, than the reading of history. The amazing story of Athens's disastrous war with the Peloponnesus not only is exciting, but also contains important lessons for any modern country that overextends itself while underestimating the ill will that foreigners have for an expanding nation, no matter how civilized. The story of the fatuous bargain Neville Chamberlain struck with Hitler in 1938 has its own grim beauty, its own utility. If Britain had stood by its ally Czechoslovakia,

Hitler might have backed down; if he did not, the war in Europe would have started one year earlier. In the latter case, Britain and her allies would have had the backing of a determined, well-equipped Czech army, Stalin might never have made the silly peace with Hitler that Chamberlain drove him to and England's example would have given a strong boost to the morale of anti-Nazi forces throughout Europe. Not the least lesson of Chamberlain's historic blunder is that the price of peace may include war at your enemy's convenience.

Still, history has practical meaning only in relation to the future; the latter is merely a continuation of the former. If this point is missed, then the reading of fiction, *any* fiction, can be equated with the study of history, which then becomes amusement, nothing more. But when history is read for instruction and as a source of insights into the future, as well as for entertainment, it becomes one of man's most fruitful avocations.

It is true that it is easier to follow history than to trace the course of the future. It is easier, too, to learn the elementary part of any subject than it is to master the whole thing. But the mere fact that it is easier does not mean that a striving for half knowledge is a better or a nobler pursuit than the search for full knowledge and understanding.

Is it a fact that the future belongs to the fifty-year-olds? A fair question, the answer to which can be simply put: The future belongs to him who takes it. Neville Chamberlain literally had the world in his hand, but he would not hold it. He permitted Hitler to take it away from him. It then remained for Winston Churchill, at sixty-six, to reach out and seize the future back for civilization. Churchill was the first leader of a major Allied power to prove he would not accept defeat passively. Roosevelt's great role as a wartime leader was made possible by Britain's Prime Minister; and Stalin, who had made his own deal with Hitler after Chamberlain's failure of leadership, finally had to be saved from the Nazis by the mighty coalition that Churchill's and Britain's courage fashioned out of nothing.

The man or woman who will not have any part of the future, who will not fight for it if necessary, will surely end up with nothing. This is as true of the thirty-year-old as it is of the person of sixty. He who shrugs his shoulders and gives up trying to shape his tomorrow, perhaps because he has arthritic knuckles, is asking in his own way for defeat.

Will he who strives for a share of the future really wind up with more than the person who does not? Yes, he will. Will he get enough more to justify the effort? Maybe, maybe not; the greater the effort, the greater the chance he will. We must never think of extra effort as if it were simply more money wagered on the toss of a coin. It is very different from that. A large bet does not change the odds on the toss, though a little extra 'oomph' to push a stalled car over the crest of a hill may make it possible to coast a mile down to a gas station and help.

There are many ways of looking at the future; two can usefully be singled out here. The first is to look at the next few decades with a view to figuring out what later historians may have to say about them. Will this approaching period of history be one of human progress? Will populations continue to skyrocket? And so on.

The second is to try to see what will happen to oneself. Given the likely trends in world and national history, what is the most interesting role I can foresee for myself? Will my present job of breadwinner or housewife be available to me, and will that job be satisfactory to me ten, fifteen, twenty years hence? Is my financial outlook acceptable? If not, what shall I do about it? And so on.

It has become trite, although it is nonetheless true, that what happens in the mountains of Peru or in central China affects all our futures. Yet how can we know what really happens in such faraway places, much less influence events there?

Should we not shrug our shoulders and say, "That is for the presidents and the premiers to worry about"?

The future of the world becomes easier to contemplate when we look at it piece by piece. Take population. In Latin America, in Africa, in Europe and in Asia, the numbers increase alarmingly. In scores of underfed nations population growth is outstripping a parallel growth in the production of food. In the United States the new people and the industries and roads to serve them are steadily spreading over the green land, each year leaving us with less and less of the well-ventilated, scenic country we once knew. It may be contended that population is only a current problem; but it exerts a decisive influence on the future. Should we nevertheless shrug our shoulders again and say, "There is nothing I can do about that; leave it to the young people, who should have better sense than to produce all those children"?

I do not seriously believe that more than one person in fifty can think in depth, and usefully, about more than two or three such vast problems. Most people, including many of the most intelligent, are incapable of dealing with even one. Yet I hold that as many as possible should make the effort, both for the good it can do for their country and the world and for the satisfactions they themselves would derive. The world could only benefit if Americans and Europeans by the millions started selecting just one world problem apiece on which they would *try* to become expert.

Take population again. A wealth of information is available to any layman who will look for it. He who will study the wonderful, awful phenomenon of human fertility will soon start to know why the number of people in India is rising so swiftly. He will learn, too, how Japan finally conquered its own postwar population boom—even though he may not approve of the method. It is not hard to become expert in this field, or at least as expert as all but the few who are paid to think about nothing else. And only ten thousand new experts on population might well develop the climate of opinion needed to avert most of the fearful revolutions and military clashes that must come if not enough is done.

To become expert on any area of national or world affairs, it is necessary to read. Read a good newspaper every day—*The New York Times,* if possible, because it has America's best coverage of world affairs. A weekly news magazine, in addition to a daily paper, can also be helpful. If you want to see something different, try a short subscription to the air edition of *The Economist,* a wonderful British weekly that covers British, American and world affairs as nothing else does.

Above all, be sure to read books. If you hear of a book you want to read, *get it immediately,* while you are in the mood, while your interest is at a peak. Do not wait for a paper edition if the book is presently available only in hard covers; get it *fast.* The reason most good intentions about reading go astray is not that people do not have time to read, but that the needed books are not purchased (or borrowed from the library) promptly, when the inclination to read them is strongest.

Magazines of opinion have their place. I suggest those who have not done so take trial subscriptions to *The Reporter* and *The New Republic,* both stimulating publications that serve an important purpose. You need not agree with the opinions expressed, but you may well find the magazines so valuable you will find the time to keep up with them anyway.

One other suggestion along the same line: Never be afraid to buy more than you read. It is far better to do this, and always have some good reading you are likely to pick up in the living room or beside your bed, than not to read at all for just one evening a month only because there is nothing that interests you in the house. At fifty years, we should realize that, aside from our health, time is the most valuable thing we have. Twenty-five or fifty dollars a year spent on magazines and books we never read is a small loss compared with the waste of a dozen evenings when we wanted something to read, but had nothing.

Each individual's own future needs thought, too. Here I would like to stress only two parts of such thought: the need to think through to a worthy long-term goal, and the need to work steadfastly toward it. Goals give life meaning, major goals give it much meaning. An unemployed bankrupt of fifty who sets out to assure himself of a retirement income of $4,000 has chosen a major goal worthy of the best of us. For him, any other goal may have to come later. But another fifty-year-old, who has substantial assets and a salary of $50,000 yearly, is making a mistake if his only goal, or his major one, is to guarantee himself an income of $25,000 a year or more after he retires. He already has security; what does he want to do, die rich? This man needs a goal worthy of his abilities. What it should be we can only guess: Perhaps to continue to perform a useful function in his business until he is ready to retire, even if not before eighty? (That is not too good an idea.) To make a second career for himself? To improve his alma mater or his community? To be of use in the fight for the conservation of America's scenic resources?

He who wants nothing and fights for nothing, gets virtually nothing—even in today's world. The wealthy man already has money; if he fights for that, and wins, he gets only what he already has. This, as he will find in his old age, is merely a special form of nothing. The average man can all too easily make the same error that older millionaires commonly fall into. Having security, he may set himself no goal at all, or he may choose a goal (such as lying on the beach at Waikiki for the rest of his life) that might be worthy of the third in command of a garbage scow, but not of many others.

Do not mistake me: I have nothing against lying on the beach. I merely assert that a plan to do so for the rest of one's life, beginning five, ten, or more years hence, is no goal worthy of a healthy reader of these pages. Yet if I felt free to do so, I would like nothing better than to go to the South Seas some time in the next few years. I'd like to stay there for quite a while, just soaking up the sun and listening to the wind in the palm trees. Three weeks or a month would suit me fine. Will you join me?

I do not mean to suggest, either, that we should *all* set out to improve the world; that would be nonsense. Knowing what you want to do, and not merely what you want to have, is half the battle. A construction foreman wants to do some deep-water fishing later on. Having only a modest bank account, he must first save up some money; then he will build his own boat. I do not sneeze at this man's major goal, and especially not if he is prepared to become a good fisherman and not just an owner of a lot of fancy equipment. Within limits, though, I am prepared to argue that the harder the goal, the better.

Let us conclude this highly moral chapter with the case of two very ordinary people who had no right to seek what they did; it was simply an unwise thing to do.

Or was it the opposite?

Mary and Fortescue Bond were tired of the suburban house they lived in. It was a small, crowded sort of place, and they had always hankered for something more spacious and airy. Beyond that, they had wanted enough land for some plain and fancy gardening and for a shade tree to sit under. But land and tree had they none. Worst of all was that the house jutted into a busy avenue along which gravel-loaded trucks thundered from morning to night.

When they were in their early fifties the Bonds decided they did not want to spend the rest of their lives in such a house. But what to do? They had only two thousand dollars saved up, the mortgage still had five years to go, and his town government salary was pegged at $7,500. But his retirement-income outlook was not bad. Fortescue figured that his pension and Social Security benefits would bring in $3,700 a year, starting when he reached sixty-five.

The Bonds decided to look into the possibility of buying the kind of place they wanted. But could they afford it? How? After paying a real-estate agency commission and paying off the mortgage, they knew they would realize roughly $12,000 cash from the sale of their present home. Their total cash would then amount to $14,000. Against this, however, the price of the sort of place they had in mind would likely be not less than $27,000.

When he checked with his bank, Fortescue found that the largest mortgage he could expect to take out was $13,500; his income was too low for the bank to go higher. So, to get their new house, the Bonds would have to invest every cent they owned; then they would have to figure on paying out close to $1,800 a year on their new mortgage, real-estate taxes, and fire insurance. Worst of all, the banker solemnly advised, was that they would be paying off the mortgage for eight years after Fortescue retired. This meant that, out of $3,700 of retirement income, they must pay $1,800 for shelter, as against a recommended ceiling of $925 in relation to their retirement income.

When the Bonds put their heads together that evening they decided the move was too risky for the present. But they had made up their minds, though they didn't quite realize it yet, that they would make it anyway, sooner or later. However, just to make things harder, Fortescue said if they undertook such a large mortgage he was going to insist on having a cash reserve of at least $3,000 from the outset. He also decided they would have to work things out in advance so that the new mortgage would be paid off by the time he was retired—or so that they would at least have to have enough cash on hand, when he reached sixty-five, to pay it off.

Fortescue's conditions might well have seemed hopeless, but from that night on, the Bonds' approach to the problem was only in terms of *how* they could lick it, not *whether* they could.

It took them just over two years to work out the solution, sell their house and move into a home they were sure they would want to keep for the rest of their lives. And when they came to make the deal, they found they had to pay not $27,000, but $30,000. How could they swing such a deal on a salary of only $7,500, and no other income? Well, they couldn't—but they got the house anyway. The dollars-and-cents explanation is shown in the table.

CASH AVAILABLE TO MARY AND FORTESCUE BOND AT TIME
OF PURCHASE OF THEIR DREAM HOUSE

Prior savings	$ 2,000
Two years' additional savings from his salary	3,000
Savings on one year of moonlighting (after tax)	1,000
Savings on Mary's earnings, for a little over one-and-a-half years (after tax)	2,000
Net cash proceeds from sale of old house	13,000*
Total Cash Available	$21,000
Less: Down payment on new house, costs of moving, etc.	17,000
Cash Reserve	$ 4,000

* Proceeds from the sale of the old house were higher than expected because the sale was made two years after the first estimate. Real-estate prices had risen between the estimate and the sale, and further payments on the mortgage had increased the Bonds' equity.

The human explanation included Mary's decision to take a part-time clerking job and hold it for six years—or longer, if she felt like doing so at the end of that time. Fortescue arranged to do some after-hours and weekend moonlighting as a cab driver; he planned to keep this up for three years. Beyond these two steps, they worked out a tight program to save as much as possible from his salary, in addition to the entire net income from their other work. Their notion, and the result proved them correct, was that there was nothing in the world they would rather do than get a nice place, and that therefore a rigid program of lean living and generous savings would be no hardship, but a delightful game—so long as they believed it would enable them to realize their dream.

No doubt the Bonds were able to buy their new house; but should they have done so? What will their situation be eight years hence, or ten years after the purchase was made, when he will be retired and the mortgage will still have another ten years to run? A second table gives the likely answer.

EXPECTED CASH SAVINGS BY THE BONDS TEN YEARS AFTER
THE PURCHASE OF THEIR DREAM HOUSE

Cash reserve forward from first table	$ 4,000
Additional savings from his regular salary—ten years at $900 (reduced from $1,500 yearly because of higher mortgage and taxes)	9,000
Savings from her wages at $1,250 yearly, after tax, for four additional years, after which she will quit	5,000
Savings on his moonlighting at $1,000 yearly for two additional years, after tax	2,000
Interest on savings accounts, after tax	5,000
Cash Savings on Retirement	$25,000*

* See the chapter "How to Sweat out an Adequate Retirement Income without Playing the Ponies" for some suggestions as to how the Bonds might plan to manage their finances after he retires. In many ways—including their $25,000 of savings—the problem described in that chapter is strikingly similar.

It is easily assumed that the Bonds would be enjoying their fifties more if they weren't still knocking themselves out to pay for a house that is larger than they need. But in fact it would be hard to find a happier, more secure couple than Mary and Fortescue Bond. Consider what they have achieved: They knew what they wanted in life, they reached out for it, they got it. The house they live in today is over 100 feet from the nearest neighbor on either side, and it stands well back from a quiet, dead-end street. They have lots of room for gardening, too, and there are some splendid maples and beeches on the property.

You will look far before you will find a happier couple than the Bonds. But you must seek even farther to find prettier flowers than they are growing right now—busy as they are.

His Name Is Legion

THE BONDS TEACH us that wonderful things can happen when people want the nearly impossible—and go after it, come hell or high water. Filled with interest and ambition, they had no need to seek goals. While their case is not unique, it may fairly represent less than a twentieth of the life histories of all Americans over fifty. Some with far lesser goals thrust upon them get along tolerably well at lower levels of achievement. Many more, it appears, lack goals beyond mere security and the right to loaf. Good as these aims are, the sum of them is clearly inadequate. Suppose the secure but goalless person finds loafing a bore—what then?

Almost any man of sixty or less knows that a weekend or a month of lovely loafing is followed by a call back to the job. Too bad to break off such delight, isn't it? Still, how many could stand a year of solid loafing, knowing all that time that nobody wants them again ever, for anything at all? Quite wonderfully, there are some who not only can stand such idleness, but actually enjoy every leisured minute of it. The point here, though, is not that some can, but that most people cannot. To bank on such delight—unless you have already sampled a year or two of straight idleness, and loved it all—is like investing all your assets in a wildcat mining stock. The gamble may pay off a hundred times over, but the odds are against it.

To better understand what this is all about, we will now consider the rather typical story of a man now retired, in good health, and financially better off than most men of his age. In certain regards our subject stands for possibly five times as many of the fifty-plus as the Bonds do.

Franklin L. was born in 1898 in Springfield, Illinois, where his father was a successful insurance salesman. In 1905 the latter was one of the first in town to own an automobile; he was an owner and driver consistently from then until his death in 1952, at the age of eighty.

The father had become dissatisfied with his arrangements in Springfield, and in 1912 he took his family to Cleveland, Ohio, where he expected to strike it rich. But for the next twenty-five years the elder L. never did so well as he had done in Springfield, although he liked Cleveland better as a place to live. In 1929, furthermore, most of the salesman's assets were lost in the stock market crash, and in the same year Mrs. L. died. The father's bad luck lasted eight years longer; but from 1938 his work prospered, so that on his death he left $30,000, after taxes, to each of his four children and a brother.

Franklin had two elder brothers and a younger sister. Michael, the eldest, had started college after the move to Cleveland, but quit in 1914 to work as a salesman for a brewery. The Volstead Act drove him from this field; from there he went on to automobile salesmanship. Thereafter Michael worked in or around Cleveland for various car agencies. He was not mechanically inclined, but he was blessed with a little of his father's flair for selling. During World War II he became unemployed and took temporary work with the city. Although these were hard times for Michael, he never dreamed of asking for help from anybody. After the war he had some difficulty getting steady work. His last regular job began in 1949 and lasted through 1954, when he was sixty. After that he held a few temporary jobs, usually lasting for no more than two or three months, and was intermittently on unemployment relief. His last employment terminated in 1957; he became eligible for old-age benefits in 1959. Michael never came under an employer's retirement plan.

As this is written, Michael, now seventy, lives by himself in a single room in Cleveland. He has no hobbies and few interests, although he sometimes goes to a Golden Age center. A brief, late marriage led to divorce in the nineteen thirties. He has no children. In fact, Michael has almost nothing beyond his $70 a month from the government and $4,000 in savings.

Franklin's other brother, Porter, was a cheerful, wild boy, who dropped out of school at fifteen, but returned to the classroom some years later. At twenty-two he entered college; six years later he had a law degree. After working for five years as a law clerk and a junior in a large firm, he set up his own practice in Minneapolis. Today there are seven attorneys in his office, and his practice is a lucrative one. There is no indication that, at sixty-nine, retirement has even occurred to Porter.

The sister, Edwina, married a building-supply salesman in 1920. Her husband, Roger G., had a territory in the Cleveland area at the time, but was subsequently persuaded to take on a larger territory in upstate New York. After an automobile accident in 1934 he decided he had had enough of the road. Taking his family with him, he moved to southern Ohio, where he wound up with a pleasant desk job in the home office of a hardware manufacturer. He was retired in 1962 on a company pension of $105 monthly. He and his wife also get Social Security benefits of $174 a month. Beyond this he receives $260 annual interest payments on savings of $6,500, while Edwina takes in $12 weekly for a room she rents to a factory hand. Their gross annual income is therefore something over $4,200.

Real-estate taxes and their mortgage, which still has three years to go, take $1,900 of this, leaving a balance of $2,300 for utilities, heat, repairs, food, doctors, clothing, and all other items. In these circumstances they are afraid to keep their house, which costs so much to run, and reluctant to sell it, for fear of what might happen to them if they became homeless.

But evidently they will hold on, because one day the mortgage will be all paid off and, what is more important, they like their neighborhood.

The $30,000 from Edwina's father was used to pay off some old debts, to make a down payment on their house, and for sundry luxuries. What is left of it is the money in the savings account and half their equity in the house.

Edwina and Roger are both engaged in volunteer activities. She works for the Methodist Church, while he helps out with the records and office work of the Y.M.C.A. and the local branch of one of the big service clubs. Their pleasures are small ones, but taking one thing with another, the G.'s are not unhappy; their only source of discontent is some healthy nervousness over a shortage of cash income.

In years gone by, Edwina gave birth to three girls. They married long ago and moved away with their husbands. One is in Los Angeles, one is in Denver, and the other is somewhere in the South. Their mother enjoys a pleasant correspondence with the daughter in Colorado.

This brings us back to Franklin, the hero of our story, who until recently was always rather hearty and outgoing. In this he was like his father; but unlike his father, Franklin has no flair for selling and no appetite for it, either.

After two years of college Franklin had decided that he was on the wrong track, and that he should learn something useful. Thereupon he left college and went into a school of accountancy, where he was judged a superior student. Upon graduation he went on to a job with a firm of accountants in Detroit; but he disliked his employers and the work they gave him. In 1925 he left Detroit and went back home to seek his father's advice. The question was, Should he go to work for another firm of accountants, or should he look for something else? His father pointed out that an accountant's training was good background for selling insurance. Why not try it? Franklin said he would think it over while he visited New York City, just to see what the place was like.

There he met and married Alice before he had a chance to give more thought to his problem. Alice instructed him to get on a payroll; the first job that offered steady pay would be best. With his ability, Franklin was bound to get ahead once he had a job. Seek money quickly, she said, and the rest will take care of itself.

Franklin sought money, and before long he found it—fifty dollars a week as a bookkeeper in the main office of a restaurant chain. Then, after a year without a raise, he shifted to a job that made better use of his skill as an accountant. This time his employer was a large paper-manufacturing company; much to Franklin's surprise he liked his new position, which paid eighty dollars a week to start. Two modest raises followed in as many years.

The L.'s had two children by the time the crash came. Now they had moved to Bergen County, New Jersey, and Franklin was a commuter. His employer stopped all hiring early in 1930; by the end of that year the firm was firing employees at all levels. Expecting to be let out at any minute, Franklin was actually relieved when the company made the first of three across-the-board salary cuts in 1931. From $4,800 in 1930 his pay shrank to $3,500 toward the end of 1932. Then in 1933 and again in 1934 he was given an enforced leave of one month without pay. Alice did not like this one little bit, but Franklin was only glad his dollars were going so much farther than they did before prices fell.

In 1929 Franklin had considered looking for a job with better pay, but the Depression had changed all that. The paper company started making a comeback in 1935; then Franklin decided to stay on indefinitely. The decision, when he had made it, gave him peace of mind; for he thoroughly enjoyed the kinds of problems he had to deal with in the course of his day-to-day work, and he wondered whether a job with any other firm would be half so interesting.

His financial progress was slow for the balance of the thirties and through the war years. At last, in 1947, he was given an important promotion and a raise to $10,000. By 1952 he had reached $12,000, and in 1958 he hit his ceiling of $13,500. He stayed on the job until his retirement, at age sixty-five, in 1963.

At the farewell party held in his honor Franklin was warmly thanked for his long and devoted service to the very best, if not the largest, paper company in America, if not in the world. His boss made a heartfelt speech, at the conclusion of which he turned to Franklin and, stuffing his foot firmly in his mouth, said, "It looks to me like you've still got a lot of good years in you, but, you know, we've all got to go sometime."

A company retirement plan had gone into effect in 1950, when Franklin was fifty-two. Because he could contribute for only thirteen years, he would get much less than the full retirement benefits for which older employees might start to become eligible in 1975, after twenty-five years of coverage. In fact, Franklin's pension came to $1,700 yearly—about one eighth of his salary. To this he could add $2,000 of Social Security benefits and $1,500 from interest and dividends on savings of $35,000. His home, worth $25,000, was free and clear. All told, then, he had $5,200 of tax-free income, and could stay where he was without paying rent. He had Alice to support, but both their boys had long since married and moved off, one to New Haven, Connecticut, and one to Long Island.

Not a bad position, you might say. But so far as Franklin could see, it was not a very good position, because Alice's tastes were somewhat expensive for their income, and so were his.

After-tax income through 1962 had been $11,800; now it was $5,200. That was a cut of more than 50 per cent. After deducting real-estate taxes, savings put aside each year (before

retirement only), costs of running the house, insurance payments, money spent on clothing, costs of his job while still
working (commutation, etcetera), he found that he had had
$6,400 left each year before retirement, and now had $3,400.
That was a cut of nearly 50 per cent.

FRANKLIN L.'s INCOME AND EXPENDITURES BEFORE AND
AFTER RETIREMENT

	Before Retirement	After Retirement
INCOME		
Salary	$13,500	$——
Interest and dividends	1,500	1,500
Pension	——	1,700
Social Security	——	2,000
Gross Income	$15,000	$5,200
OUTGO		
Less: New York State* and Federal income tax	3,200	——
	$11,800	$5,200
Less: Life insurance, health insurance, Social Security tax, savings, and contributions to company retirement fund	2,750	——
	$ 9,050	$5,200
Less: Commutation and lunches in city	750	——
	$ 8,300	$5,200
Less: Expenses for household insurance, real-estate taxes, utilities, fuel, lawn mowing, snow removal, and repairs to house	1,900	1,800
	$ 6,400	$3,400
Less: Food, car, and medical expenses	3,200	2,700
EVERYTHING ELSE	$ 3,200	$ 700

* Although the L.'s live in New Jersey, Franklin's job was in New
York, and he had to pay income tax there.

Before retirement he and Alice had spent $3,200 yearly for the big items of car expense, food, doctors, and drugs. These items simply had to be cut now, and Franklin arbitrarily sliced them to $2,700 by reducing car expense. Before retirement these outlays had left him with $3,200. Now that he was no longer working, and had cut them, he was left with only $700. This was the unkindest cut of all.

It meant that the L.'s could now spend only twenty-two cents for each dollar they formerly laid out for vacations, liquor, tobacco, magazines, newspapers, movies, laundry, dry cleaning, haircuts, beauty treatments, charities, and other sundries—including Christmas presents for the grandchildren.

Franklin had retired in February, but it was not until April that the L.'s were trying for the first time to face the truth, which was that despite all his training in money matters they were going to have to live a life they had not planned for. For example, they would not be able to take even one of the big trips they had dreamed about. In fact, they could not take even a modest vacation without cutting into their savings and thereby slicing their income.

There was at least one way in which that income might be raised. This was to put some of his liquid assets into annuities. But Franklin had considered such a plan and rejected it because he wanted to keep $15,000 in savings accounts, for emergencies, and the balance of $20,000 in common stocks as a hedge against inflation.

You might think that, with his accountant's training, Franklin should have been financially prepared for the situation in which he now found himself. In a way he was. Most men of sixty-five and more who live with their wives have incomes of under $2,900, and perhaps only one couple in five gets as much as Franklin's $5,200. And nearly all older couples with incomes as high as Franklin's include at least one employed member. Financially, the L.'s were well ahead of almost all nonworking couples of their age.

But it is still true that Franklin had failed to face his problem squarely. He had not thought through the personal, day-to-day adjustments he would have to make after he lost his job. He had gone so far as to say, "This is the best money arrangement I can make. When the time comes we'll just have to get along on what we get."

That far and no farther. Now he and Alice would have to sit tight and take the consequences.

Alice had a few friends in town—not many—with whom they could visit back and forth for dinner or an occasional game of bridge. They could watch television any time they chose, and they could go to the movies once a week if they felt like it. The theater and other New York amusements were 'out.'

Almost immediately there were little troubles the L.'s had not foreseen. You might say they were old troubles; certainly none of them was really new. Yet, now that Franklin was idle, these petty annoyances he used to shrug off became magnified out of due proportion. "An idle brain," says an old proverb, "is the devil's workshop."

For one thing, Alice and Franklin had always had different ideas about television shows; but now, for the first time, her choice of programs got under his skin. He thought them stupid and nagged at her because of them. Somehow his nagging gave Alice the idea he picked *his* shows simply to annoy her. Visiting with friends was another source of annoyance. Mostly, Franklin thought Alice's friends as stupid as her television shows. Grumbling, he would go along anyway, or put up with the guests when they came to the L.'s house. There was not much socializing anyway; and if Alice got something out of it, well and good. But Franklin's new discontent was contagious, and soon Alice became as bored as he did whenever they dined with friends or played bridge.

In recent years the street the L.'s lived on had filled up with young couples and their small children. Franklin thought their new neighbors self-centered, which was all right because, being more self-centered himself, he wanted nothing to do with them anyway. But to their children he was an old fusspot. He did not want the kids stepping on *his* lawn or peering into *his* garage; in fact, he just wished they would all go away. They wished he would go away, too. After an early-April storm Franklin was struck on the cheek by a snowball thrown by one of the children.

The movies were a disappointment. The newspapers and magazines described quite a number of films they would both have enjoyed, but hardly any of the best were booked into the local theaters. From the end of January to June the L.'s went to only three movies. Of these, Alice enjoyed the first, they both liked the second, and they both hated the third.

Since the old P.T.A. days it had never occurred to either of them to take an interest in community activities; they shared a fine contempt for 'do-gooders' and prided themselves on their ability to stand on their own feet. If they could do it, why couldn't others? And if others could, where was the need for community work? So the L.'s reasoned.

So Franklin's little problems were that he was dissatisfied with television, with the movies, with his street, and with visiting back and forth. Still another little problem was that he really did not have any interests beyond reading the newspapers. Or was this a big problem—*the* big problem?

As Alice saw things, he would not be fidgeting around all day if there were not something seriously the matter with him. Was it his health? Or was it that the day was twenty-four hours long and Franklin had no good way to use more than half of that time?

Sitting at home one night in May, Franklin thought he felt he would explode if things followed their present course for one more day. "Let's go to Europe," he said. "I have plenty of money in the bank. The change will do us good—give us a chance to think things over." It wasn't a bad idea, but in their situation it was just patchwork. And Franklin knew it.

In June the L.'s were off on a conducted tour that took them to Rome, Naples, Florence, Venice, Vienna, Zurich, Geneva, Paris, Berlin, Copenhagen, Amsterdam, Brussels, London, Stratford-on-Avon, Edinburgh, and Dublin. Eight weeks and over three thousand dollars later they were back home, and it was still 1963—August 10, 1963, to be exact. And the cost of the trip had cut their income by $130 a year.

It took three weeks to tell their friends about the highlights of the tour and to show the pictures they had taken. Then the L.'s visited their children's families, in turn, and repeated the performance for each.

Now what?

They still needed a vacation, but now it was a vacation from each other that was necessary. Franklin hit on the idea of spending some more of his savings on a trip to Minneapolis to visit his brother Porter, whom he had not seen since the thirties. Alice could visit her sister in California. So in mid-October they went their separate ways, on the understanding they would come back home in one month.

Franklin had arranged to stop off twice on his way west, to see his brother Michael and then his sister. Michael's poverty and idleness shocked him deeply, but he was more disturbed by his own failure to find anything to discuss with the former car salesman. He kept wanting to ask Michael what he was up to, but the evidence was all too plain: Michael was up to nothing whatever. When his brother asked what *he* was doing, Franklin could only answer that he was on his way to see Edwina and Porter.

The visit with Edwina went differently. Lunch was waiting when he reached her house, shortly after noon. Over the main course the three of them—Edwina, Roger and Franklin—had a spirited conversation about old times. Then, over the apple pie and coffee, his sister asked Franklin what he planned to do, now that he was retired. Instead of answering, Franklin talked about his trip to Europe. After lunch his sister apologized because she had been unable to put off a meeting with a group of younger women at her house. They were members of a church committee to which Edwina belonged; the committee was reaching the climax of a drive to raise money for a new organ. She suggested Franklin and Roger might visit together upstairs while she met with the ladies in the parlor.

Upstairs in his den, Roger told Franklin about the work of his club, which for the past several years had been raising money to help crippled children. Now the club had embarked on an educational program to improve public understanding of the mentally ill. Roger recommended that Franklin join his local chapter of the club to see if he could get it going on a similar program.

By the time he flew off to Minneapolis, late in the afternoon, Franklin made up his mind that Edwina and Roger were not his sort of people. When you came right down to it, they were little better than run-of-the-mill do-gooders. Porter would be different.

Franklin got a warm reception in Minneapolis, and the two brothers talked far into the night. The lawyer had been to Europe several times, so they had common ground there as well as in their childhood. Next day they visited Porter's offices, where Franklin was introduced to the partners and to several secretaries. It was later, over lunch, that the conversation started to drag for the first time. They had touched on national politics, but found they disagreed on almost everything in that sphere. Porter tried to save the day by discussing some of his more interesting cases; for a while the attempt seemed successful, but gradually Franklin was filled with a secret resentment: It was not fitting that Porter should be so immersed in his work while he, Franklin, was here to visit with him.

By the next day the brothers were reduced to exchanging pleasantries, and within a week Franklin ran off to Florida to see whether it would not be a good idea to move down that way. After all, many retired people did just that. There must be a reason.

There was a reason, of course, but he was in too black a mood to see it. He looked briefly at some real estate, but the two properties he checked were far too expensive, and the cost of selling and moving would be prohibitive—so he told himself.

So, after only two weeks' absence, he arrived back in New Jersey. The house, as he approached it, looked cheerless; the weather being chilly, he found it cool inside. Soon he had the heat turned up. While the furnace did its work, he lay down on his bed, pulled up a blanket, and took a nap. When he awoke it was midafternoon, and the house was comfortable. He made himself some tea. As he drank it, he decided it was just as well he had come home ahead of Alice. Perhaps if he could just sit still, all by himself, he would be able to think his problem through.

During the next several days he sat still quite a bit, and he strolled around the neighborhood somewhat more. He also paced the floor. Soon he was eliminating some false notions that had been bothering him. He discovered, to his surprise, that money had nothing to do with his problem. Franklin made this finding one day as he tried to figure out how much difference a thousand dollars' additional income would make. Try as he would, he could not see that it would make any difference whatever. True, he and Alice could go to the theater in New York, and they might be able to travel a little bit without reducing their savings; but a thousand dollars could amuse them for no more than a couple of months out of the year. How about the other ten months? Anyway, the extra income was not in sight.

Suppose he could locate a desirable, less expensive property in Florida? Surely, life *could* be cheaper there, and it would be pleasant to lie in the sun with nothing to do and nothing to worry about. Why not? For a while he had himself believing Florida was the answer to everything; then, suddenly, he knew he would just as soon move to Greenland, provided only that there was *something interesting to do* there.

Just something to fill the God-awful days—that was all he wanted. Something he could throw himself into. Florida would be a fine place to have something to do, but he had no connections there. Nor did he know what he could do in Florida that he could not do in New Jersey. Or in Tasmania. Somehow, just understanding his problem a little better made him feel good.

Franklin went for a stroll one fine, leaf-smoky day in November. As he walked, he thought over and over: Not money, but something to do; not money, but something to do. But *what* to do?

On his way back he was nearing his house when he noticed a group of boys looking for something under the cars parked along the curb. Maybe it was that ball, right beside him, in the bushes. He stooped and picked it up. "Catch, somebody," he called, as he tossed it in the general direction of the children. A big boy caught it.

For a moment the boys looked incredulous. Then one of them thought to thank him; two or three smiled. As he walked into his house, Franklin felt more at peace with himself and the world than he had in months, and he knew why. He had done a little something for somebody else. His services were appreciated, and they would be welcome again any time. He would have something to tell Alice when she came home; those kids weren't such a bad lot after all.

It was Oliver Wendell Holmes who said that a moment's insight is sometimes worth a life's experience. That little episode with the ball in the bush gave Franklin an insight he had lacked for the first sixty-five years of his life. Now, at last, he saw he had to be needed, to be appreciated, to be wanted—call it what you will. He saw that if he had no role in the lives of others, if he could not somehow be of service, he must always be at loose ends. But given a job to do, and somebody to appreciate it, he could be as happy as a lark. And it didn't much matter whether the job was a big one or a little one.

When Alice finally came back to New Jersey she was so pleased by the look she saw in Franklin's eye she was sure he must have enjoyed every minute of his visit to Minneapolis. It took a while for him to convince her he had never been so miserable, and then to tell her, so that she could understand, exactly what he had found out about himself and what he intended to do about it. Not only had he decided to go back to work—at first she thought this notion stark insanity—but he even suggested they start being neighborhood do-gooders. Alice's first tack was to try to humor Franklin for his funny new ideas, but so contagious was his enthusiasm that she soon found herself trying to improve on them. Finally she adopted them as her own.

There is more to the story of Franklin and Alice L., but we can afford to leave them here. Plainly, a happy ending is possible. For Franklin sees his problem now, and he has the means to beat it. His hand is firm, his knowledge of accounting is sound. He will take a brush-up course in accounting for small businesses; then he will try to pick up a little part-time accounting work in the stores around Englewood. His short-range goal will be to net up to $2,000 a year. Working and studying will occupy his mind, and the money—even half of $2,000—would begin to provide enough for vacations and occasional evenings in New York.

In the long run—well, what is the long run, anyway, except a lot of short runs put together? Especially if you have something to occupy your mind and nobody can fire you or retire you.

There will be other changes made, too. The L.'s will try to make friends with some of the young parents on the street, and they will throw their house open to some of the young children for a little while on Saturday afternoons. As Franklin says, children and 'young marrieds' are people, just like everybody else.

Will Franklin's dreams come true? Maybe, maybe not; but I am inclined to think they will. For, as his former boss said, Franklin still has a lot of good years left in him. And he has money—ample money, really—and he knows where he wants to go.

My chapter title suggests that Franklin L.'s name is Legion. The quotation from the book of St. Mark is, "My name is Legion; for we are many."

The Art of Thinking Small

THE OTHER DAY I overheard a lady ask a tobacconist how many cigarettes she could safely smoke each day. "I'm sorry, m'am," the merchant replied, "I wouldn't know that. Some can smoke a lot, some can smoke only a few, and some shouldn't smoke any."

What is the smallest amount of income you will need for happy retirement?

I'm sorry, dear reader, I don't know you well enough to answer that question. Some need more, some need less. But just tell me who you are, how and where you live, what your dream of happiness is, and I guarantee I'll come within $1.89 of the correct figure, provided there is enough money in the world to open your particular door to happiness.

It is trite, but true, that nobody can buy happiness. All money can do is open a door; after that, it's up to each of us to go through the open doorway to seek his own version of felicity.

"Aha!" someone says. "Never mind who I am; just tell me the minimum price of opening the door."

The Department of Labor has some information of value here. Figures it assembled in 1959 show the cost of "a modest but adequate" level of living for retired couples in a number of cities from coast to coast. The figures allow for a limited amount of entertainment, the rental of a two- or three-room apartment, and $300, more or less, for medical expenses. Here are the totals:

South: Atlanta, $2,720; Houston, $2,641.

East: Baltimore, $2,840; Boston, $3,304; Cincinnati,

$2,925; Cleveland, $3,244; New York, $3,044; Philadelphia, $2,909; Pittsburgh, $3,102; Scranton, $2,681; Washington, $3,047.

Central: Chicago, $3,366; Detroit, $3,096; Kansas City, Mo., $3,034; Minneapolis, $3,135; St. Louis, $3,099.

West: Los Angeles, $3,111; Portland, Ore., $3,049; San Francisco, $3,223; Seattle, $3,252.

Between 1959 and late 1964, the average cost of living rose by about 6 per cent. So, to each of the above figures we must add roughly $200 to find the annual cost of living for a retired couple. A revised, rounded figure for Atlanta, therefore, might be $2,900; for New York, $3,250; for Los Angeles, $3,300; for Seattle, $3,450; and so on.

(Since the above was written, the Community Council of Greater New York has released up-to-date figures for that city. They show that retired couples there should now have a net income of $62.14 weekly, or $3,231 yearly, to live up to the same standard. This is just $19 a year less than our estimate!)

Can people be happy on less money than the figures the Department of Labor gives for a "modest but adequate" standard of living?

Most certainly they can; but just how much less money we do not know, in general. As additional dollars are shaved from already-low budgets, we must know more and more about the individuals involved if we are to predict what the chances are that their little money can open the door to happiness for them.

But, believe it or not, $2,000 can open it, in some special cases. Even today.

How can this be? Take the case, if you will, of Norah and Gordon Fox, living outside an Iowa city of 40,000 population. The Foxes, both pushing seventy, have their health, keen intelligence, and a cash income of $2,050 from Social Security and other sources. Gordon is a former jack-of-all trades, and master of most of them. A good deal of his working life, particularly the latter part of it, was spent in small factories, where he was always welcome because of his dexterity and his know-how with many basic types of machinery.

When the second of their two daughters got married and moved to Oregon ten years ago, Mrs. Fox took the first job she had held since she was a girl; she went to work in a retail bakery, where she stayed on for five years, while Gordon worked at various jobs in factories and repair shops. The Foxes' cash savings of $5,000 come from Norah's earnings.

They bought their home, with its three acres of land, before 1940, and by 1960 the mortgage was paid off; now they own the place free and clear. There are two outbuildings for the few chickens they keep and for the tools, which are well used, because the Foxes run a quarter-acre vegetable garden. The chickens and the garden and a few fruit trees provide non-monetary income worth over $300 yearly.

They also have other nonmonetary income. Norah makes all her own clothes at a saving of $80 a year. And there is hardly a thing that goes wrong with their car, a 1954 model with a manual gearshift, that Gordon can't fix himself—except for an occasional worn-out tire, which he trades in for an in-expensive recap. Gordon also makes all the little repairs around the house, whether in the basement or on the roof.

"What!" I hear somebody exclaim. "Don't tell me a man of seventy climbs up on the roof." The best answer to that is Gordon's own: "Nowadays it's cheaper to fall off the roof and break your neck than it is to hire a roofer. Besides, it's kind of nice up there. From up on the ridge you can see clear to the other side of town."

Here is how the Foxes spend their cash income:

Food	$ 550
Taxes and insurance on home	300
Medical	300
Clothing	120
Car, including insurance	260
Fuel, electricity, phone	340
All other	180
Total	$2,050

A joker in the Fox budget is the item for medical expense, which has actually been running around $50. But the $300 outlay is as rigidly controlled as any item on the list; Norah insists on putting $25 a month aside for this account. The part that is not spent goes into the bank, in a separate "get well" account that amounts to $1,400. The "all others" items is lean. Out of it must come all entertainment (unless occasional drives in the car are called entertainment), hardware, subscriptions, charity, and so forth.

The Foxes are not worriers, but they are great penny pinchers. No barber or beauty parlor has gotten a nickel from them since Gordon last worked for wages, five years ago; Norah cuts his hair and takes care of her own, but to look at them you would guess they both had had their hair improved in town five minutes ago. Their car has to last them a long time, so Gordon will not drive on icy or snowy roads that have been salted. He knows if he did so the old car, neat as a new penny today, would soon rust away.

Gordon has a friend in the beef-fattening business whom he visits once a week. When he is with the friend he often helps out by repairing some of the machinery on the farm. Early each spring the friend shows up at the Fox place with some farm equipment. When he leaves, a little later, the garden is ready for seeding. "It beats spading," Gordon says.

The money value of all the things Norah and Gordon do for themselves, such as running the garden, caring for the hens, sewing, and repairing the car and the house, amounts to about $600. So the Foxes live as well as an equally prudent, but less handy, home-owning couple with an income of $2,650.

Although their cash income is fixed, the Foxes have two hedges against inflation. One is home ownership; no landlord can raise the rent on them. The other hedge is all the things they do for themselves; the price of these will not rise. Still, inflation is the chief threat to their security. Their Social

Security checks will not increase as prices mount, nor will the interest on their savings.

They have some ideas about what to do to meet inflation. One plan is to take in a roomer, probably a schoolteacher. Gordon thinks they might also put up a small rental house on the back of the property. "But not yet," he says. "We'll jump off that bridge when we come to it."

Federal Old Age Insurance, home ownership, their savings, hard work, good health and a sense of humor have opened the door to happiness for the Foxes. They enjoy being busy on their land and in their home, they are amused by some of the radio and television programs they tune in on, they are active in church and community work, they like to visit around with friends and relations. The Foxes got where they are because they have long made a habit out of happiness and because they have enjoyed working hard to make ends meet. Their secure little income and some modest savings help to give them the courage to stand on their own feet, as they have done in the past.

There is a message for millions of Americans in this story. It is that the door to felicity can be opened with little more than a monthly Social Security check. But when the available money is that meager, it may take some real ability and zest for work to pass on through the open door to the pleasant living and pride of achievement that lie beyond.

The story of Franklin L. suggests that money without purpose can leave a couple as high and dry as retirement without money. The Foxes teach that insufficient money for comfortable retirement can provide inner drives that make up for inadequate pensions and that these drives can give life some of the meaning it should have for all of us, all our lives.

Many people would rightly hesitate to try such a strenuous cure for too little income after sixty-five. The life the Foxes lead is an active one and, while Gordon does not mind the hard work he does today, he may not enjoy it so much after seventy-five. But by then the Foxes may have taken in a roomer; or perhaps they will have put up and rented that small house Gordon is thinking about. Either move, or both of them, would provide more cash income and so make life easier.

How to Sweat Out an Adequate Retirement Income Without Playing the Ponies

MANY COUPLES in their fifties face the prospect of a retirement income, including Social Security benefits, of less than $2,500. Of these, the majority who are now assured of at least $1,500 yearly can raise their after-sixty-five income to $3,000. Some may fail to go higher, while others will find it challenging and even pleasant to push on beyond the $4,000 mark.

Let us take as an illustration the case of Emery and Goldie Orr, both now fifty-five. Emery's past employment record has been spotty, but his prospects for steady work are now good. His income is $8,700. Because of his uneven earnings in the past and the costs of supporting and educating their only youngster, he has no money in the bank; and no company pension awaits Emery. But the Orrs' son is on his own now, and they have no significant debts beyond the mortgage on their home, which will be paid off by the time they are sixty-five. Emery figures their Social Security benefits at $2,300 yearly, beginning in ten years, when he will quit work.

If the Orrs will put $2,000 yearly into savings, they will have a $25,000 nest egg available on his retirement. Through the magic of interest, the $20,000 they put away will have been augmented by $5,000, assuming the rate to be a stable 4 per cent.

What effect would this have? Very simply (too simply, as we shall see), the $25,000 at interest would add $1,000 to their $2,300 of Social Security income; so the total income would be $3,300.

"Fine," you say, "but can they really save as much as $2,000 a year out of a gross income of $8,700?"

They can. Let us remember those figures put out by the Department of Labor indicating that in the typical larger American city a retired couple can live on a "modest but adequate" level for $3,250, on which they pay no tax. The Orrs, of course, are not retired, they must pay income tax, and their living expenses run much higher than $3,250.

Let us assume the Orrs have $800 of tax deductions for interest on their mortgage and tax on the house, and that further deductions come to $300. We can now estimate their Federal taxes at $1,270 after the tax cuts of 1964. Including utilities, they must also shell out, until the mortgage is paid, about $1,700 a year for heat and shelter, against the $925 the renting city couple pays. A further difference of perhaps $800 should be allowed for Mr. Orr's travel to work and lunches and incidentals.

Using the budget of the retired city couple as a starting point, we therefore find that the Orrs' yearly expenses and savings might work out as follows, *provided they start now to save an amount that must be close to a reasonable maximum:*

Modest but adequate budget of retired city couple	$3,250
Add: The Orrs' Federal taxes	1,270
Costs of the Orrs' shelter beyond those of city couple	775
Emery's work-connected costs of travel and so forth	800
The Orrs' annual savings	2,000
Subtotal	$8,095
Not budgeted	605
TOTAL—The Orrs' annual income	$8,700

To understand this budget, we must know the items in the Department of Labor's 1959 budget for the retired city couple, as adjusted to the present, averaged and rounded off by us. These are: Food and beverages, including alcoholic beverages, $940; rent, heat, and utilities, $925; clothing, $230; medical care, $330; transportation, $175; other goods and services, $650. In the Orrs' budget, life insurance and state income tax, if any, would have to come out of the $605 difference between their income and the total of the items listed in their budget.

How would our calculations be affected if the Orrs were now fifty, instead of fifty-five, and were to start their program of savings immediately? In that case they could get exactly the same result ($25,000 of cash saved up at age sixty-five) by putting away $1,200 a year, instead of $2,000.

At any earlier time of life it would seem almost impossible for a couple to save nearly a quarter of an income in the range of $8,500. Aside from the costs of child rearing, younger couples in the suburbs and elsewhere feel the need to stay in the swim, to keep up with the Joneses, and to hold their position in the rat race. But in their fifties people often find they need not respond to such pressures; many have already backed off from mere social competition without even planning to do so.

For example: In our fifties we no longer need to buy a car every two or three years, even if that has been our custom down to now. Nor do we need to own a big car, whose only advantage is that it is as long as the Joneses' monstrosity and maybe a little longer. A Volkswagen or the somewhat larger Swedish Volvo will do as well; both are inexpensive to buy, cost less to run and to repair than conventional American cars, last much longer, and are always in style—because the manufacturers refuse to play Detroit's game of outdating last year's car by replacing it with a heavily advertised later model that is rarely better than last year's, and may be worse.

When retirement comes, how well off would the Orrs be in

comparison with the city couple living on $3,250? We are now assuming, remember, that their $25,000 would earn 4 per cent, or $1,000 yearly.

In most parts of the country they would likely be somewhat worse off than their city cousins. With their mortgage paid off, Emery and Goldie might spend about $900 yearly for shelter, or a trifle less than the city people pay for their apartment. On the other hand, the city couple's $175 for transportation is too low for the suburbs; if the Orrs owned a car they could expect difficulty in holding expenses for gas, oil, depreciation, repairs, insurance and licenses under $400.* These differences suggest the Orrs might need $3,450 to live on the same scale as the urban couple. But Goldie and Emery would have only $3,300, and we have not allowed a margin of safety for inflation. What to do?

I suggest that they might put $15,000 of their savings into annuities when they reach sixty-five. If they purchase two annuities of a certain type, costing $7,500 each, one hers, one his, they can be assured of as much as $1,125 of annuity income as long as they both live. Whichever outlives the other would continue to get about half that. Here is their revised income situation so long as both are living:

Annuities	$1,125
Interest on $10,000 savings	400
Social Security	2,300
TOTAL TAX-FREE INCOME	$3,825

Presto! Without gambling in Wall Street they have raised their guaranteed income by $525, while keeping a liquid sum of $10,000 free for emergencies.

Since we are doing some supposing, let us now suppose the Orrs decide to sell their home, as many older people do, when Emery quits work. Let's say the house brings $21,000

* In the Orrs' preretirement budget $225 of this item of expense was included in Emery's $800 for travel, etc.

after costs of sale, and that they put $11,000 of the proceeds into savings and $10,000 into two more annuities, one hers, one his. Here, then, is the new picture:

Income from $25,000 in annuities	$1,875
Interest on $21,000 of savings	840
Social Security income	2,300
TOTAL TAX-FREE INCOME	$5,015

Not bad, is it, when you consider that when Emery was fifty-five he was wondering how he could scrape together enough to raise his retirement income from $2,300 to $3,000?

Assuming the Orrs sell their home and manage their money as suggested, they will be free to do almost anything they wish. They can, for instance, move to the city and live there at well above the "modest but adequate" level described by the Department of Labor, and they can still have enough left over to put about $1,000 yearly into travel or whatever else strikes their fancy. If they tire of this life, they can move almost anywhere in the United States—or abroad—and rent a house or apartment for as long as they like. They can even buy another house in one of the retirement areas, although in this case they should have kept about $25,000 in cash, instead of $21,000, in order to have a good liquid reserve after paying for the house.*

Another thought for the Orrs, if they are not bent on complete retirement, is to start working *now*, when they are fifty-five, toward some kind of independent or semi-independent employment that stands a good chance of producing $500 to $2,000 of yearly income after Emery retires from his job. Assuming they stick to their savings program, the advantages

* Note that we have not gone into such questions as what happens after Emery or Goldie dies, or any of several other important financial matters. The reason we have not is that we have just one purpose here: to show that inadequate assets can usually be increased by conservative action and managed so as to produce an adequate retirement income.

to them of *earning* additional income after sixty-five may be summarized as follows:

> The increased income is guaranteed to make life more enjoyable.
>
> Income that is worked for independently is generally inflation proof. The more inflation, the more free-lance workers charge for their trouble. (Home ownership is another type of hedge against inflation; so are common stocks. Annuities, Social Security, and interest on savings offer no such protection.)
>
> Postretirement work—both as goal and as activity— adds zest and purpose to life; it reduces or eliminates the shock of retirement for men.
>
> Work, including postretirement work, puts us in touch with people. The contacts made through it are valuable to our lives as social animals.

But while it is often wise to plan on earning money after sixty-five, it is not a good idea, at this stage of life, to become tied down to anything. Much wiser to have work to do, but be able to quit when we please! The person who is not ready for full retirement at sixty-five may find he has had enough one year or five years later. What fun to be able to retire at will then, *when he wants to,* instead of being obliged to quit forever at sixty-five, when his employer tells him he must!

How the Wizard
and the Good Fairy
Saved the Unwise Man
from an Uncertain Doom

POSTRETIREMENT WORK can be a wonderful thing in a man's life; but it is rarely wonderful if it enslaves him whom it is supposed to liberate from want or boredom. Many a dream for the years after sixty-five has been ruined because a retired man has unwisely taken on the whole responsibility for a small, demanding business, such as a gas station or a retail store. People who know nothing whatever about retailing often imagine it to be a pleasant and easy occupation, dependent only on a lazy offering of merchandise of a kind people buy. But beginning retailers soon discover that the public is a hard taskmaster, that the door must always be kept open during business hours, and that creditors want their bills paid on time, whether or not business is good.

In Florida—and other retirement centers—there are retired men without relevant experience, who have bought gas stations in the belief that any fool can make money working a gas pump. Such people normally go out of business in a short time; they learn to their sorrow that only some fools can make money that way. Mostly, the successful gas station operators are fools with quite a bit of experience, and aren't fools after all.

At least one retirement book suggests that retired people can prudently go into bookselling, after looking into it a bit. But confidential figures sent to retail subscribers to the credit services of Dun & Bradstreet indicated, not too long ago, that bookstores were the second most hazardous of many types of listed retail businesses; only gift shops were riskier. If to the outsider the good bookstore seems pleasant and easy to run, that is because it has to seem that way; otherwise people will not patronize it. Behind the façade of easy graciousness the successful bookshop is a complex operation that constantly strives to match up tens of thousands of book titles with the faces and the tastes of thousands of customers. If books and customers cannot be matched, the business fails; often it fails anyway, because the cost of matching up becomes too high, or for any of a number of other reasons.

I mention bookstores because they are so appealing to men and women who do not know how to invest their money or their time. There was, for example, a Wisconsin newspaper executive who had always liked to be surrounded by good books, but who had never had experience retailing books or anything else. When he reached sixty-five he wrote the proprietor of a small, Midwestern bookstore in a city of 100,000 population, explaining his situation and asking whether the owner would like to sell his business. Many months later the two struck a bargain, and the formerly retired man took the business over and began to run it.

Before its sale the store had passed the $50,000-a-year mark. Discounts averaged 40 per cent. At this level the owner could take out $6,000 a year for his investment and his toil. The growth rate was 8 per cent yearly. On the record, then, there was every reason to believe that within five years the store would be doing over $70,000 of business. On such sales an owner-manager could take out $10,000.

The new owner was determined not to change the business in any way. It soon turned out, however, that he was taking better care of his merchandise than he was of his customers. For example, it sometimes happened that when a prospective buyer picked up a book to look at it, and then put it down again, the new owner would come over and line the book up with the others on the counter while the customer was still standing there. This made the customer uneasy. As old customers shifted their trade to a competitor, they told one another that whenever they were in the store they had the feeling the proprietor was watching them constantly.

If a customer asked, "Do you have such-and-such a book," the new owner would often say, "No." What he should always have said was, "I don't have it in stock today, but I would be happy to get it for you. May I do that?"

To protect the new owner from the high-pressure sales methods of an overzealous competitor, a publisher's representative had warned him that overbuying was one of the most serious mistakes of beginning booksellers. So the proprietor bought too little, with the result that the quality and the quantity of his inventory steadily declined. This was fine with him, because he counted it a victory to have less stock at the end of a month than he had at the beginning. But the smaller his inventory, the fewer customers he could please, and the less business he did.

The shop was now run to suit its proprietor's pleasure and pride of possession, not the convenience and delight of its customers. Bookstores commonly bear the stamp of their owners' taste in books, but this store now reeked of its owner's taste in tobacco. The new owner's most damaging achievement was to make his customers feel the shop was merely an extension of his cigar.

But even as the old customers began to learn that the store was no longer for them, the new owner learned, to his regret, that it wasn't his dish either. The steady grind of paper work, the browsers (especially the dirty-fingered children) who bought nothing, the nine-to-six, six-days-a-week nursing along of a declining business—all soon palled on him. Most painful of all, perhaps, was his belated realization that he had none of the good retailer's patience or instinct for service.

At the end of his first year he found he had done only $35,000 of business, when he should have done $54,000. But the result was even worse than these figures suggest, because the rate at which he did business had declined steadily throughout the year, so that by the end of the year he was actually selling books at a rate of only $25,000 annually. Now he had a simple choice to make: He could hang onto an ailing, money-losing business; he could sell out, provided he could find a buyer; or he could close up shop. It takes years to build up a retail book business, but very little time to wreck one.

A wizard and a good fairy stood between this business fiasco and a human tragedy. The wizard was the new owner himself; he had spent most of a lifetime building up a retirement income of $15,000, and he had accumulated considerable liquid assets. So he could, if he chose, lock the door and take his licking without impairing his security. He was really no fool; or even at the very worst he was a wise and prudent fool.

The good fairy appeared in the guise of a chain of bookstores that had once offered to buy out the original owner. The man at the head of the chain knew the store well, and felt a profitable unit could be set up there. So the corporate good fairy bought out the faltering wizard just in time, and in less than a year had built the store's trade up to where it had been before; and now it is pushing on beyond.

Surprisingly enough, therefore, the wizard got out of the bookstore in firm possession of his shirt and trousers. The worst that happened to him was that he spent a full year as a slave to the petty details and long hours of a small store. Happy as he was when he moved into his own little bookshop, he was even happier when he moved out.

His Eye Is on the Floor

LIFE BEGINS AT FIFTY for planners-ahead, for many of the creative, for most of the self-employed, and for still others. If I speak much about the self-employed, it is because the man who works for himself often makes a superior adjustment to old age. A few salaried people of fifty or so, recognizing the advantages of self-employment, may still be able to benefit from this lesson by becoming their own bosses. Others, now self-employed, may reconsider a decision to get on a payroll for the apparent security such a change might offer.

The majority of salaried people, tied down by rigid retirement plans and properly unwilling to make a hazardous change to self-employment, can nevertheless learn something of value from the lesson taught by the man who is his own boss. Finally, some who are safely on the pay lists of employers with flexible retirement plans may elect to take their pensions at sixty-two instead of sixty-five, or at fifty-eight instead of sixty-two, in order to start early on a low-pressure, second career—a career in which they will work for their own sweet selves, but at a minimum of risk.

The better part of our lesson is that the *man who knows he has to work things out for himself often does so*. Franklin L. had to find his own answers, too; but the security of his job kept him from understanding the hardest question until he was retired. Then the shock of having to find the answer so quickly put him on the right track—though it might easily have broken him.

Another part of the lesson is that the aging self-employed

can change their patterns of life earlier or later than employees can, to meet their individual needs, and can also do so gradually, thereby avoiding the shock of abrupt change from full-time employment to idleness. Quitting your job slowly may be impossible if you work for somebody else; but it is often the best way. And it is also the most natural way in the world if you are your own boss. For the self-employed man, arrival at the age of sixty-five brings no shock. Getting there finally is pretty much like reaching fifty-eight or seventy-three—it depends on how he feels that day. And how he feels does not depend on which birthday it is.

Consider now the case of one Martin A., a fair example of a self-boss working outside the highly trained professional fields such as the law, architecture and medicine. Our subject is, in fact, a rough modern equivalent of Meyer Mueller, the nineteenth-century Pennsylvania Dutch farmer.

There were nine million self-employed people in this country in 1962, including over two and a half million farmers. But Martin is not a farmer. His business is flooring, and if you are interested in almost any type of flooring or floor covering, whether composition, carpeting, tile, terrazzo, linoleum, or what have you, Martin A. is a good bet. His business is not based on his having a large inventory, on his location (he is on a side street in a growing city of 80,000), or on the quality of the flooring materials he stocks—although he has very high-grade flooring along with other less elegant and less durable types. When you come down to it, he is known best for his good advice and his considerate service.

Martin, who is about fifty, got into the flooring business eighteen years ago, shortly after he came out of the Coast Guard. Before the war he had worked at a lumberyard where some floor coverings were carried. There he had noticed that quite a few sales were lost because the range of samples was too small. Other prospective deals went down the drain because his employer gave his customers too little help, preferring to run his floor-covering department the way he did his lumber business, on the cafeteria principle. But Martin soon realized that many customers wanted the different types of coverings evaluated, wanted estimates, and did not know where to find building-trades workers who would be qualified to lay the hard-to-handle types of material.

In 1946, with eight thousand dollars in the bank, stars in his eyes, and his heart in his throat, Martin took the plunge. He rented a showroom and dry storage space in the basement. He laid in as many samples as he could get his hands on, put in a limited stock of popular items, took space in the classified section of the telephone directory for his own city and two adjoining communities, and started running a tiny display advertisement in the local newspaper. He informed all the area contractors and builders that he was ready to do subcontracting work, he notified the city that he was interested in bidding on reflooring jobs, and wherever he saw construction work he found out who was doing it and introduced himself.

It was a tight squeeze. For three years he had to take on afterhours odd jobs just to keep afloat. For six months of that time he worked nine hours a night as watchman on a school construction project. Reporting on the job at eight in the evening he worked through until five in the morning, when his relief came on. He made a point of packing a good meal, which he ate just before he went off duty. That way he could go straight to bed when he got home at five-fifteen. At quarter to eight he got up again, and by quarter to nine he was back in his display room. When Meriam, his wife, relieved him at noon he would go home to the hot lunch waiting for him in the oven. Then he would sleep for just over an hour and return to the store by two. He locked up at five, went home for another meal, then piled into bed for an hour and forty minutes of shut-eye. At eight he was back on the job at the construction site. So, during the week he got just five and a quarter hours of sleep each twenty-four hours. But Saturday nights he slept twice as long.

Meriam earned a little money, too. After her three children were packed off to school she would uncover her typewriter and start working on the typing jobs she had collected. To get this work, she ran classified ads from time to time in the newspaper; but most of it came in from people who already knew she gave good service and charged reasonable rates. Most weeks she could count on twenty dollars' worth of work; she had no time for more.

In those early years Martin's worst times came when he was asked to bid on big jobs. With these there was always the danger that the work might be spread over long periods during which he would get no pay; and meanwhile his costs, for labor and materials, would steadily rise. And there was another danger, too. If his bid was low enough to get a big job, he had to face the possibility of loss. Martin simply did not have the capital or credit to take such chances, even though the probable profit would otherwise have justified the small risk.

In his fourth year, after he had backed away from five such jobs, and taken two others, Martin was approached one day by an out-of-towner named Frisbee, who said he was going to build a huge industrial and office structure and wanted Martin to bid on supplying and laying the flooring for the whole building.

"I'm sorry," Martin replied, "but I can't help you. I don't have the capital or the credit to swing that type of job. Why not try Scanlon?"

"Because I've talked with Scanlon, and I don't like him. People here tell me you know your business and give an honest value. You bid on this, figure on bank interest, and I'll see that one of the banks gives you any loan you might need if the bid is good. If necessary, I'll cosign your note."

"No," said Martin. "If I bid too low I could take more loss than I've got capital. Then how do I pay off my loan? So if I bid, I'll have to play it safe by going so high you'll need to give the contract to somebody else. I've been all over the problem before, and I know I can't afford to take a job like this. It's too big for me."

Frisbee rapped his knuckles on the desk. "Look here," he said, "if you want this job you can probably get it; and you know enough about the business so that you ought to make a fair profit off it; though I warn you a high bid won't take it. But if you'll agree to put in your bid, I'll sit down with you or your lawyer and work out a guarantee against your taking more than a thousand-dollar loss if you get the award. Take it or leave it. What do you say?"

"I say I never fought so hard against making a sale before in my life, and I'm about ready to give in. You send me the bid forms when they're ready, work up the guarantee against loss and send that along too, and I'll take a crack at it. I can use the business."

Frisbee frowned. He told Martin that there was a joker in the deal. The fact was, he explained, that he was damned if he knew how to draw up the specifications. "I've put up a few buildings in my time," he said, "but I've never encountered the kind of flooring problem we're going to have in this one. The foot and freight traffic will be heavy in a lot of the areas; we are going to have to expect grease getting on the floors; we'll have to study the effects of some strong chemicals that might get loose, and on top of all that the joint is supposed to look as bright as a new penny all the time. The directors want to use the building as a model factory to impress big shots from around the country and from Europe. If you want to work with me you're going to have to help draw up the specifications."

Frisbee was no simpleton. He knew that Martin could not supply all the information that would be needed. But he also knew that ample free consultive services were available to dealers, architects and others who had flooring problems. True, such service is always biased, because it is paid for by manufacturers trying to sell their own wares; but at the same time Frisbee was sure that Martin himself was unbiased and had the brains to use the free services and the background and gumption to evaluate them. So Frisbee had little doubt he and Martin together could eventually reach the right answers.

It took five months to get the specifications drawn up and approved. Having been in on the contract preparations, Martin was in a good position to make a close bid, but in the end a competitor from another city bid a little lower. Frisbee, judging the difference too slight to matter, saw that Martin got the job anyway, on the ground that he would probably turn out a better grade of work.

When the contract was completed, a year and a half later, Martin figured he had earned $4,000 for his own time plus a profit of $7,000. It was not a mountain of money, but the project was a sensational turning point in his business. There were many reasons for this. One was that it made him a welcome user of bank credit, so that he was never again in the position of having to turn business down for want of cash. Another was that it added to his capital, enabling him to take more risks in the future. It also helped him secure exclusive dealerships on two prestige lines of material. Along with six other contractors, his name was put on a bronze plaque in the reception room of the new building. Because the floors were both attractive and serviceable, this turned out to be one of his best advertisements, bringing him other industrial business and even some requests for consultation, at a fee. Furthermore, the story of his negotiation with Frisbee became local legend. The point of the legend is that if you are good at your business, even if you have no capital, you can win out through sheer perseverance.

There is some merit to this conclusion. Though the proof of his success came in the dramatic deal with Frisbee, Martin's greater achievement was earlier—otherwise Frisbee never would have known him by reputation, and never could have come to him. So while Frisbee provided an important assist, it was Martin who was responsible for his own ultimate success, which he would have realized just as surely, though more slowly, if there had been no Frisbee.

Martin's net income averages $15,000. He has two steady employees: A girl Friday for the showroom and a man who runs the delivery truck, who is good at estimating small jobs, and who can check on the progress of contract work. The man can also lay down most types of flooring. He gets a good wage and a small share of the profit on any business he finds.

Most of the contract work is done by day workers in the building trades. No work, no pay. If he ever had to do so, Martin could lay off his two employees and go back to running the business with Meriam. Beyond this, he has figured that he could even close up his showroom and, by keeping up his contacts with contractors and architects in his part of the state, clear $5,000 a year on consulting work alone. With various odd jobs, and the prospect that Meriam could always earn a little if necessary, he believes the two of them could keep their work income up to $8,000 under the worst circumstances he can foresee, short of his becoming an invalid.

Martin's security goes beyond this. He is fully covered by Social Security, and in 1953 he started making payments to a retirement annuity fund that will pay him $125 monthly for life from the age of sixty-five. He also has savings of $18,000, and he figures that by holding on to his earnings of 4 per cent on his savings, and adding $1,000 yearly from his other income, he will have accumulated $52,000 in cash by his sixty-fifth birthday. Martin believes that if he were to retire then, and could not sell his business, he could still count on a cash income of $5,900 from interest, his annuity and Social Security. Before then his home will be free and clear, so that it seems to him that he and his wife would be able to get along comfortably enough.

There is in the United States a thin scattering of salaried

people who can count on a postretirement income of $8,000; and there are even a few who can anticipate $10,000 and up. Some of these, measuring their retirement income against Martin's $5,900 when he reaches the magic age, may feel sorry for him.

If so, they had better shift their pity to some other object; for Martin has no intention of retiring at sixty-five. He has simply used sixty-five as a convenient point from which to figure what he would get *if he had to retire*. But his health is good, he enjoys his work, he likes to earn money, and he does not work for a company that will force his retirement whether he is ready or not. So, right now Martin thinks he would like to retire when he reaches seventy-two; even after that he expects to go on indefinitely earning $2,000 a year as a consultant.

From Martin's own plans, and from what we know about the general picture for aging persons, we can put together a horoscope for his next thirty years. First, we can agree with Martin that he will work, pretty much as he is now doing, until he reaches seventy-two. His financial position at sixty-five will be about as he pictures it, and in the seven years from then until seventy-two his business will net him only slightly less than it does now—about $13,000 annually on a larger volume of sales, but with increased help, so that he can work at a slower pace.

At seventy-two he will discover, as many doctors, lawyers, farmers and other self-employed people have done before him, that he has no particular reason to retire at that time. And so he will keep on as before, for another four years, until age seventy-six, and during these years he will still take $13,000 annually out of the business. Then he will sell the good will and physical assets, lock, stock and barrel, for $60,000. After taxes and other costs of sale, Martin will have $50,000 to add to his savings, which will rise thereby from $124,000 to $174,-000.

"Whoa," you say. "Wait just a little bit there! How will he raise his savings from $52,000 to $124,000 in only eleven years, on a net business income of $13,000? What is he, a financial wizard?"

Not at all. Martin is just a persistent, self-employed wizard, and not very different from a lot of other self-employed wizards. Here is how he will increase his savings by $72,000 in the eleven years from sixty-five to seventy-six:

First, he will continue to save $1,000 yearly from his business earnings for eleven years	$11,000
Second, he will contribute his entire annuity income of $1,500 yearly to his savings, for eleven years	$16,500
Third, he will contribute his entire Social Security income, from age seventy-two until seventy-six, amounting to $2,280 yearly for four years	$ 9,120
Fourth, his interest at 4 per cent,* figured to be compounded annually, will total	$35,250
Add his savings to age sixty-five	$52,000
	$123,870

* Note that Martin distrusts investments in businesses he does not control. That is why all his savings go into savings accounts, and none into stocks.

To round this off to $124,000 he needs only to write a check for $130 on his checking account, which he keeps at $2,000.

Of course, Martin will have to pay taxes on his salary, on the interest on his savings, and on a portion of the $1,500 annuity money he puts into his savings each year. But the Social Security income will be tax-free, and he and his wife will each count for two exemptions, because of their age. The upshot, during the years from sixty-five to seventy-six, will be that, on the average, Martin and Meriam will have about $9,000 spending money, after taxes, even allowing for some increase from present rates. From the moment Martin sells his business and stops adding to his savings, he will still have $9,500 yearly of spending money, or $3,600 more than he would have if he were to quit at sixty-five.

For the fifteen years from sixty-five to eighty, Martin will have a total of $136,000 of money to spend, aside from what he will add to his savings in the first eleven years of that period. Furthermore, he will have a liquid fund that will reach a peak of $174,000 on which he can draw if his spendable income should prove inadequate in an emergency. Three striking advantages of Martin's position from sixty-five to seventy-six are his freedom of access to substantial funds; a business income that will provide excellent insurance against inflation, as Social Security, savings, annuities and pension systems do not; and the right not to retire until *he* decides the time has come.

Our crystal ball tells us that Martin and Meriam will each have one major illness before he retires. At fifty-nine, Martin will experience a mild coronary, which will keep him away from business for four months and will cost two thousand dollars.* Martin will pay for this by cleaning out his checking account. Four years later Meriam will require major abdominal surgery, and because diagnosis will have been delayed, the experience will be hard on Meriam and very expensive—five thousand dollars, all told. Again Martin will clean out his checking account, and now he will have to invade his savings to the tune of three thousand dollars. And he will repay the money borrowed from savings, although it will take him three years to do so.

Does Martin save too much money and use too little? Can he lead a good life on what he is spending? To get some perspective on this question, consider that in 1960 only 13 per cent of all American families and unattached individuals had

* There is no fixed price for coronaries; some cost much less than the amount mentioned, some more.

an after-tax income of $10,000 or more,* while Martin has $10,500 left after taxes, after his $1,000 contribution to his savings fund, and after his payment on his annuity. Out of this $10,500—and the other $10,500's of the past several years— Martin has been putting aside $1,000 more for the education of his children, and Meriam has been adding $500 to this from the $1,000, before taxes, that her typing still brings in. When this program is completed, three years hence, it will have put one girl through three years of college and their son through medical school. The girl who went to college will have left to be married, and the girl who did not go is already married and the mother of two children.

Is the story of Martin A. a truly singular success story? Not really, though his financial circumstances have become far better than those of the average American. Martin's income is more typical of the self-employed than it is of other groups. Figures for 1960, the latest available as I write, show that, on the average, families of the self-employed earn more than any other group, including families of managers. And, of course, many self-employed people continue at their work beyond sixty-five.

Perhaps only one family in ten has as much spending money as Martin and Meriam; among those that have, not one in three has the financial and emotional security which Martin's dogged independence has brought to his family. So if we were to construct a contentment or happiness index for the entire population of the United States, we might find the A.'s somewhere in the top 3 per cent. For a guess, only 1,500,000 families are as well off, everything considered.

Looking back on Martin's life from his eightieth birthday, thirty years hence, we will be able to say that his career has revealed a pleasant but not highly unusual combination of

* Source: Department of Commerce, Office of Business Economics, *Survey of Current Business*, April 1962, as quoted in the 83d edition of *Statistical Abstract of the United States*.

140 LIFE BEGINS AT FIFTY

three fairly common details in American biography: self-employment, good health and prudence. After all, if Martin were extraordinary he would be earning not $15,000 but $35,-000 or more today; and from here on his income would continue to rise swiftly as he maneuvered his way through lumberyards, real estate, construction businesses, gravel pits and what have you. The striking thing about Martin, really, is not that he is so unusual but that he is so ordinary.

When he reaches eighty, Martin will be ready to go to his maker a whole man who has done what he wanted to do, and has done it well. He will have been retired only four years at that age, but he will have enjoyed life more than any of his acquaintances. Having pursued independent interests down to seventy-six, he will never be at a loss after that; and he will rejoice that he need never sponge on anybody and will be able to leave his children something for their own old age—which will be coming along surprisingly soon.

The Parable of
the Reluctant Dentist
and the Carolina Parakeet

MY DENTIST for several years was a lively, part-time ornithologist whom we will call Pierre, though that was not his name. A fine, if unenthusiastic dentist, Pierre was a storyteller of rare excellence. His technique was to seat you in his chair, plug your mouth with gadgets, and start to work with his drills and his talk.

It was in the chair of Pierre that I first heard of the important ornithological business of counting the feathers of dead birds, and it was there that I found out about the migratory habits of the American and the European robin. But the most memorable tale Pierre ever told was about the once-abundant Carolina parakeet, a large, gaily colored bird that, down to the middle of the last century, ranged as far north as New York State. The Carolina parakeet is extinct today, so now there is no big tropical bird to be seen north of Dixie.

The final chapter in the life story of this wonderful bird contains a lesson for men, women and children of all ages; that lesson is: *Never do anything merely because 'everybody's doing it.'* Do not speculate in Wall Street simply because the barber and the hairdresser are doing it. Do not retire fully and completely just because that is what your cousin George will do. Do not move to Florida or Arizona merely because everybody's doing it. Do not commit yourself to working after sixty-five just because I or somebody else tells you it is a good thing to do. Think first about *what you want and what you are capable of;* decide what is wisest; then do what is truly best for yourself—even if it means being different from everybody you know.

Read now the sad tale of the Carolina parakeet, which got along well enough with the American Indian, but not with the white man. For it was the possessive white man who first planted apple orchards in the land, and, like Eve, the parakeets thought the apple the most tempting thing that had ever been invented. Each fall, as the apples ripened, the happy robbers would descend on the white man's orchards in flocks of twenty-five or more. Being big birds, they could ruin the fruit on an entire tree in a matter of minutes.

If the farmer chanced not to see the flashy marauders as they settled, he was almost sure to hear them, for the Carolina parakeet was a gossip whose chatter was heard far and wide. Now alerted, the farmer ran for his old smooth-bore and his shot and his powder. Soon he was in the orchard with his trusty blunderbuss at the ready.

Bang! Down fell a Carolina parakeet. Whoosh! Up flew the other birds. Then, as the farmer added powder and shot to his civilizer, the wheeling beauties started to cry over the unkind fate that had taken their comrade from them. Soon one of the mourners came flying down to join the fallen hero, and all the others circled in behind.

Bang! Another Carolina parakeet bit the dust. Whoosh! Again the startled flock flew up and away, and again the patient farmer bent to his task of readying the weapon. Once more the birds wept piteously for their loved ones; once more they followed a faithful leader down to the side of the dead.

Bang! Whoosh! Bang! Whoosh! Bang! Whoosh! Bang! And so on until not one member of the flock was left alive.

This story, retold ten thousand times, is the reason you cannot today see a single Carolina parakeet in a single zoo or in

Carolina or anywhere else. Weep with me, reader, for that gorgeous, amiable bird that has gone the way of the passenger pigeon, the dodo, and the bustle—a senseless victim of group-taste and group-think.

In his early middle age, at a time when other dentists were dutifully filling more and more teeth, my friend Pierre was filling fewer and fewer. But unlike the more eager students of bicuspid and molar, Pierre was counting more bird feathers than you could shake a stick at. Soon he stopped filling teeth altogether, and became a full-time ornithologist on the staff of a museum of natural history. That was what he wanted to be, and that is what he became.

Weep, oh weep for the imitative parakeet, but weep not for Pierre, who went his own way even as the dentists-at-heart went theirs.

The Swing of the Pendulum

FOR NEARLY ALL OF US, each day has its peaks and valleys of productivity. For example, one man—a physicist engaged in research—starts work at eight in the morning, reaches top performance by ten; in the following two hours his efficiency gradually drops off. After lunch his output rarely approaches its morning peak, though it may rise again in the evening if he chooses to work then. A sensible person who is free to do so will adjust his work habits to such individual patterns of productivity, reserving the easier jobs for his periods of least efficiency.

Beyond the daily swings from high output to drowsiness, from near elation to semidepression, there are longer cycles, lasting days, weeks, months and even years. Not uncommonly, we find ourselves at a low point of interest and energy when we suffer from a cold, when we have a lingering infection, or some other nagging malady. Oftentimes it is fruitless to ask which came first, the discomfort or the depression. Whichever it was, it makes good sense to stick to the practice of attacking the physical problem first. When this is licked we may already be past the phase of depression. If not, there is time enough to consider other possibilities; in fact, we may feel there is too much time. For depression and worry may only lead on to more of the same, and all this mental futility can consume tremendous amounts of time and energy.

It is at our own peril that we allow ourselves simply to accept the low points of emotional and energy cycles without responding to them in a directed manner. Taking a trip, seeing a doctor for a complete physical check-up if we have not had one in the past year, taking long walks, reading Ian Fleming, Mark Twain, James Thurber, William L. Shirer, or whomever else we enjoy—these are just a few of the things we can do as opening moves to accommodate, to forget, or to fight a prolonged depression.

Man survives because he is the particular *active* creature he is; the most cerebral member of the animal kingdom, he is still infinitely more monkey than God. So, like the monkey, the important thing oftentimes is to swing smartly through the trees, or at least *do something,* whether one thinks of the action taken as accommodation, diagnosis, cure, escape or exercise.

The alternative to action may be unhappy daydreaming or empty brooding. Brood along with me for a moment about all the miseries people have; would you not agree that a catalog of these creature discomforts, in all their forms, would rival the Chicago telephone directory in size? True, hardly any of these agonies would be peculiar to people who are fifty or more, and most of them would appear trivial or dull to anyone who has not experienced them. But just think of the quantitative mass of mammalian misery such a directory would represent! Think of all those thousands of people who went to bed feeling well last night and woke up this morning with the first symptoms of their last ailment!

Think too, if you are minded to, of all those who woke up this morning with a stiff neck.

So what? Should we be indiscriminately concerned with the ailments of a lot of fools, geniuses, millionaires, and beggars? Of course we should not; nor should we be constantly concerned with the probability that one or all of these discomforts will strike us now or in the future.

If we wish to be idiotic we could make a companion directory to the delights of all the American people. It, too, would be a giant book; and it would be equally worthless. It would have no bearing on my case or yours.

Indeed, this whole line is futile, except insofar as it helps to point up the uselessness of empty worrying—the sort a man does when he says to himself, "Fred Jones was taken to the hospital with leukemia just six years ago, and today I can't seem to wake up. I wonder if that's what is the matter with me."*

Western man responds better to activity, to challenge, to change, than he does to a life of idle contemplation. Changes in his environment, changes in his occupation, enlargement of his point of view as by reading books, having new experiences, traveling, meeting interesting people and becoming friends with them: All these are stimulating and good for him.

Like water trapped in a swamp some go stale if they stay in one place, or in one narrowly defined job, or in one situation too long. The same view out the window, the same contacts with the same things at the same time of every day, the same work at the same desk day after day, the identical problems to solve, month in and month out, year after year; these, we know, are things that make people go stale. The more monotonous and the less challenging one's daily work and life, the more stultifying the result. And the effect is worse on people of superior sensitivity than on others.

At the age of fifty the likelihood of mental slackness is at a high level. Its signs are many. They include boredom, lack of

---

* I am intrigued by those people who never *seem* to have any of the ups-and-downs which I detect in myself and most others. Some are perpetually cheerful, while there are others whose unhappiness for today is exceeded only by their misery over the awful events they foresee for tomorrow. A woman I know provides an illustration. When you meet her on the street and say, "How are you?" she will answer *invariably* by showing you a bruise on her leg, by telling about a fit of coughing she had last night, or perhaps by relating how she suffered this morning when she spilled a cup of hot coffee on her lap. This lady is educated, articulate and intelligent, and you would expect her to know better. But I am afraid that with her it is not just a question of etiquette; it seems she is genuinely depressed by these things, *always* depressed. Still, better manners might help! Nowadays when I meet her I say "Hello, nice day," or something else that provides less of an opening for a medical case history.

interest in job, family, home, or friends, lackadaisicality, and so forth. To friends and family, people who have gone stale because of too much routine may seem duller and less interesting than they once were. Some may affect a hollow gaiety.

Is it possible, on the printed page, to strike a blow against staleness?* The most we can do is to offer some fresh thoughts, suggestions, and asides for the stimulation and guidance of the aware. Of the two, stimulation is the more urgently needed; for guidance without stimulation is like a steering wheel and an empty gas tank. So let's go, with or without a steering wheel, but preferably with!

Variety comes close to the essence of all the pleasantly meaningful aspects of our lives. We all depend on a variety of foods to make our meals palatable. For breakfast, a woman may consume some bread (itself made of a number of foods), butter, fruit jam, sugar, coffee, orange juice. By eating a variety of foods of her own choice, she enjoys her meal infinitely more than she would if she were obliged to eat only one kind—even if she were allowed to choose which food that might be. From her breakfast menu it follows that a variety of occupations exist. There are dairymen and orange farmers, there are those who pick coffee in Brazil, those who grow wheat in the American West, those who plant sugar cane in the Dominican Republic, and those who tend plum orchards in California. There are railroaders, food processors, advertising copy writers, wholesalers, retailers, and many others on whom the lady depends for her varied breakfast. While it is interesting to think of all the people who make such a meal possible, it would be even more so to go and see them at their work.

As with food, so with clothing. If we had nothing to wear but white sneakers, some of us might look a little better than we do. But since there is a wide range of clothing to choose

---

* I assume the absence of serious ill-health and deep-seated problems requiring the attention of a physician. The rule is, when in doubt, see your doctor.

from we find people choosing clothes to cover their nakedness, to insulate their bodies from the cold, to suit their different personalities, to pamper their changing moods, and to attract the opposite sex. The constant changing of style and the variety of acceptable clothing within the limits of a given style help keep people happy. To supply all these clothes there are cotton growers in the American South, silkworm growers in Japan, textile workers in Italy, England, New England, and elsewhere, and there are multitudes of processors, designers, wholesalers and clothiers. In clothing, as in food, the apparent and hidden varieties of things are beyond counting.

As with food and clothing, so with people and ideas; friends and ideas that appeal to us one day may pall on us the next. At such times we must leave these people and these paths of thought, so that when we return to them we will like them better than ever before. Our lives need to be cheered and informed by a variety of friends and ideas.

The same might be said about possessions. Probably there is not much wrong with the old car in the garage, the old phonograph in the living room, or the unread books on the shelves. Yet how refreshing it can be to buy and own a new car, a new record player, a new book!

In fact, then, *we need a variety of varieties.* In each of the following areas changes and contrasts frequently brighten our days and enrich our lives: clothing, food, friends, ideas, place, employment, climate, weather, entertainment, books, news, color, sound, challenge, activity, smell, shape, texture, and so on.

But variety can play us false. Many changes may seem merely strange or bizarre, and therefore not close enough to what we understand or are familiar with. Change must somehow be relevant; a new hobby must not be something suited only to a gorilla physique and a baboon intelligence. A new book, containing a new idea, must be within the grasp of our intelligence, and it must be on a subject that interests us. And it had better not be written in Uzbek. The new friend we have sought out must not be a completely inarticulate bore.

Although we are not gods, and cannot enjoy the occupations of gods, the more ground we include within our frame of reference, the more meaningful variety we can find in life and the more we enjoy living. If our point of view is severely limited, like that of the monkey, so is our capacity to discover a variety of things suitable to our outlook, and so is our ability to steer ourselves out of the doldrums when we drift into them. To enjoy variety—and hence life—to the fullest, we should always strive to broaden our outlook on life. Each little success here adds meaning and interest to another slice of our world. Each success makes us less chimpanzee and more human—perhaps even more godlike.

Yet a limited point of view is often one of its holder's proudest possessions. Dreadful examples are found among boosters of all kinds, including religious zealots, whether Mohammedan or Christian, and rabid patriots, whether Russian or American. But for each of these people there are many others who have a very limited view of things only because they have always, by habit or force of circumstances, trodden a narrow path. Enthusiastic about nothing, they commonly fear additions to their field of vision as much as any zealot.

At any given time our readiness for enjoyment is indeed limited by the breadth and depth of our view of life; but it is wrong to assume that everybody has his point of view and is stuck with it. It is wrong, first, in that it assumes a person is limited to seeing things from one angle only. As we shall see later on, there are ways in which a point of view can be drastically changed.

The assumption is also wrong in that it commonly includes the further, hidden assumption that breadth of perception and depth of view are also fixed, along with point of view, and not subject to alteration. We can accept this assumption easily enough (too easily, that is) in the case of people who are socially remote from us, who perhaps live in primitive lands where everybody is illiterate and the sole occupation is selling feathers to tourists. But when we look at familiar situations we find much that is wanting in the concept. Consider the American shift away from isolationism in response to the shocks of Hitler and of nuclear weaponry. Isolationism is a symptom of a limited view of man and society, while the global approach reflects a broader outlook.

A more startling instance of a mass broadening of outlook came in the wake of the firing of Sputnik I on October 4, 1957, when millions had their eyes opened to some important facts they had theretofore overlooked. We learned quickly that America was not always first in science and technology. We learned, too, that dictatorships are not necessarily incapable of technological leadership. We found out that a limited scientific and military conquest of space might be possible.

Having seen these facts, millions of Americans beheld their country in a new and deeper perspective. For the first time they understood how the United States could become a second-rate power or no power at all. They saw at least part of the connection between education on all levels, on the one hand, and national achievement and national survival, on the other. Interestingly, there was little that was new in all that was then learned; for there was at least a handful of people in this country who knew in 1956 every one of the facts which became common knowledge only toward the end of 1957; every fact, that is, except the startling one of the Soviet achievement with Sputnik. But the rest of us were not ready to believe these few informed people. It required the shock of this Soviet 'first' to enlighten the rest of us.

Not the smallest result of our new perception was a dramatic stepping up of efforts to educate superior high-school students. Another result was an overhauling of much of American education from the earliest levels through high school. This review and reorganization of the schools is continuing. The results have startled the colleges, where teachers have seen an astounding improvement in the readiness of entering freshmen. Now the colleges find they must overhaul themselves if they are to challenge these accomplished young Americans, who owe their fine preparatory education to Mr. Khrushchev and his Sputnik.

It seems, too, that shock, or something like shock, can broaden any individual's view of things. Just for example, a nearby disaster or a death in the family can help us to see ourselves and our uncertain span of life in a setting that is truer than the overly secure, day-to-day existence that most Americans experience for much of their lives and which we like to believe is the standard, normal, expected thing.

But shock isn't always necessary. A knothole in a board fence provides a poor youngster with an excellent view of one pair of goal posts on a football field; from this vantage point the lucky boy can even see some touchdowns. But while the view through the knothole may be fine for a ten-year-old, it can be awfully boring for the man who wants to see all the complex plays and action the game has to offer. So, later in life the boy at the fence steps from the knothole to the box office for a seat on the fifty-yard line. From there his view is so much broader that he can follow every play on the field, including the key ones that lead up to the touchdowns.

The broader our outlook, the more variety we can take in, and the more interesting life becomes. And we *can* broaden our outlook at will—as a rule.

The View from the Cradle — and Elsewhere

IT IS A FACT, too, that our point of view changes with time. The newborn infant sees things differently from his not-yet-born twin, and finds the view from out here not entirely to his liking. Food and air, formerly provided by an excellent natural arrangement, now have to be sought out and fought for. To get what one wants is a struggle, and one often has to raise one's voice. Really, the service is quite impossible compared with what was once expected as a matter of course. That younger twin, not yet born, still has all the best things of life available to him. Ah, to be young again!

At about the age of six there are two points of view worth mentioning. Youngsters starting off to school are sometimes delighted to have reached the age at which new mysteries of the grown-up world are revealed to them almost daily. A little boy, aware of the heavy responsibility suddenly thrust upon him, marches off to kindergarten just the way Daddy marches off to his office, with his papers tucked under his arm, his marbles in his left fist, and a peanut-butter sandwich in his hip pocket. At the end of the day, when Daddy comes home, the boy finds it easy to sympathize with the old boy. After all, we're all in this thing together, he reasons, and studying your letters (A, B, C, and so on), fighting off the girls, and trying to walk on your hands is hard work, say what you will. No wonder Daddy is tired!

Another viewpoint typical of six-year-olds is that of the

crybaby who feels that being sent to school simply amounts to being sent away from home and mother. The things you learn in school are worthless, the other kids are pests, the food is no good, you can't take your favorite blanket to school, you can't go home when you please (which is all the time), and the teacher is a jail keeper. Ahead, the child sees only more and more school, more and more rejection by his parents. A youngster who feels this way, if he knew how, might paraphrase General Sherman's famous words, uttered at another institution of learning: "I am sick and tired of school," he might say. "Its glory is all moonshine. . . . School is hell."

Ten to twelve is often an age of frustration. The boy who was so happy to be almost grown up at six is now bursting with anger or overcome with ennui at the realization that, after all these years and after trying so hard, he *still* is not fully grown up, and will not be for years and years. He falls on his face when skiing, he doesn't know how to repair the TV, the teacher tells him his handwriting is no good, his ball-point pen won't write on grease, the carbon paper in the typewriter is *always* wrong side around, and to top it all he gets a fishhook stuck in the seat of his pants just where he can't see it. Why does everything have to happen to him?

At fourteen one boy's feet get in his way, one girl's glasses get in her way, and kids of ten or twelve get in everybody's way. ("Gee," says one fourteen-year-old to another, "do you remember when you were a kid of ten, and how easy school was, and how much fun you had? Little kids today are spoiled. They only know how to be pests, not how to have fun.")

One sensitive fourteen-year-old, whose parents have gone broke because of a shaky investment, perceives that the world has fallen in on him. He believes he will not be able to finish high school, college will be out of the question, and while others are having fun or succeeding in the things of this world, he will be forced to live by the sweat of his brow. He believes his lot will always be cold shivers at dawn and hard labor through the long, hot day. His tender years confer no blessing on him, because in his immature view they only mean he has that much longer to endure the tortures of life before he finds the painful release of a lonely death.

Eighteen to twenty is often an age of preoccupation. One person of this age is preoccupied with his studies, another with the excitement and novelty of his first real job, and another is preoccupied with sex, or at least with the opposite sex. To each of these three exquisitely concentrated people it is only what they are now doing that truly matters in life. The fellow who is studying so hard is the same one who at fourteen thought he would have to work at dumb labor for the rest of his life. You see, some unforeseeable circumstances have intervened, including a slight betterment in his parents' finances and a fine scholarship in recognition of his diligence, his limited means and his intelligence.

One youth of eighteen to twenty is trying to ban the bomb, another is writing poetry, and another is disassembling a 1931 Buick or a 1927 Franklin (and perhaps trying to complete a 1926 Marmon with the parts). Meanwhile, a classmate is doing volunteer work for the new nations of Africa or perhaps is collecting all the known and unknown phonograph records made by Duke Ellington through 1936. A bearded twenty-year-old is busily exposing the Philistinism of all who work for a living. Just a few years later the fellow with the beard has become the pleasant, tidy clerk at the next desk. The poet has become an advertising copy writer, the student of sex the first father in his block, the college student a teacher, the bomb-banner a budding Lion, and so forth.

Gerontologists point out that the older we get, the slower we age. This sheds light on the declining frequency of changes in point of view after maturity. But while the circumstances of life also change less rapidly after twenty-five or thirty, they go on changing nevertheless. It is in good measure the slowed-down aging process and the less rapid changes in our relationships to family, job, and so forth, that lead us into the commoner changes in point of view when youth is gone.

The fellow who had the beard, and then became the clerk at the next desk, assumes executive duties later on. Through circumstances, and because he is a sharp cookie, he eventually becomes boss of an entire office; as boss he takes on a senior executive's point of view. The advertising copy writer, on the other hand, remains a copy writer for life—and enjoys his work thoroughly. The man who was once such an avid student of the opposite sex, and then the proud young father, at fifty has become so interested in religion and morality that he will soon be named a vestryman of his church and an adviser to the police department on the problems of youth.

But it is not alone advancement of age that brings about changes in point of view; new information may have the same result. Someone who told a twenty-year-old that tinkering with old cars was pure damn foolishness might himself be character- ized as a fool by the youth one day and looked up to as a demi- god the next, when the young man learns that the object of his contempt is a poet, a Duke Ellington fan, a Friend of Nigeria, or all three at once. Indeed, heroes and villains are frequently interchangeable, depending on where you stand and when you look at them.

It is hard to give too much stress to the importance of this everyday fact of the shifting point of view, for it is partly our view of life that gives tone and meaning to our existence, and that gives us our identity. Important, too, for people thinking about their own lives is the fact that it may be possible to change one's point of view through an act of will. This can be achieved by drastic action, as by changing one's job, selling one's business, walking out on the family, or moving to Aus- tralia. Fortunately, there are people who have demonstrated the possibility of making such a change without resort to such extreme measures. Among the milder devices we may mention the reading of books (not just any books), moving to another house, or consciously taking a new and a more or less responsible approach to everyday work and decisions.

Among mature people, changes in point of view probably happen quite frequently in a way something like that which occurred in the case of Franklin L., whose story is related elsewhere. Here the changes were, first, from a settled point of view (that of a staff accountant with a paper company) to that of a displaced person (one who had no life or activities or plans outside his job, and who was retired from his job in this condition). Franklin L.'s loss of his anchor and identity first drove him into a panic. But being a levelheaded man, he fought his way out of this and started to think. In the course of thinking he saw that he had to be needed, and that the best way to be needed was to make friends with his neighbors and to find a low-key occupation in which he would be his own boss. A course of events beyond his control had driven him from his job and from his employee outlook. His subsequent adoption of a badly needed new point of view did not just happen, nor did he find it in a vacuum.

The Two Fates

DEEP DOWN, there are many who still believe in a fate that rules our lives. This man is a lawyer, and having had a good practice in Hartford for many years, he has come to accept this occupation and this city as part of his fate. That man, the proprietor of a successful retail business in Tulsa, cannot think beyond his store and the possibility of moving it next door. He too is fated—not just by the fact of being in the retail trade, but because his business is a success. If it failed, he would be fated to do something else.

What irony! The successful men appear to be the slaves of their successes, while the failures are set free by their mistakes.

This is illusion. The prosperous man has the means to be freer of economic and social restraint than the fellow who could not make it up the hill; the failure is governed by an economic necessity a hundred times as urgent as that which besets the success. It is another question whether the latter has the inclination, the wit, or the courage to use his greater freedom. In a sense, anyway, both are slaves to fate. But fate is in their minds only, and is a movable, changeable thing over which they have great power—if they only knew it.

Do I seem to be saying that we are individually the masters of our separate fates? If so, I had better explain myself. The concept of fate is so diffuse, so subject to shifting definition that, at a minimum, it should be broken down into two distinct words. Then, and only then, should we try to decide whether or not we have any true power over it at all. I suggest that one of the two words be written "fate," in the usual way. The second we can write "Fate," always with a capital first letter.

It is our little-*f* fate that we are born of our parents, that we are black or white, that we are Americans or Albanians, that we are raised in a farming or an urban society, that we are gifted with second sight or are sightless from birth. This fate is the real McCoy. It means that we are all going to die one day, we know not when. Mr. Hugh G. Flood, a ninety-four-year-old denizen of the Fulton Fish Market, in New York City, once showed a fine appreciation of the larger meaning of fate in his answer to an intolerant young white man from Alabama who had seen Flood, a former drinking companion, eating and being friendly with Peter Stetson, a Negro. "You're a troublemaker," the young Southerner had said. "What race do you belong to, anyhow?"

"The human race," Mr. Flood said. "I come from the womb and I'm bound for the tomb, the same as you, the same as King George the Six, the same as Johnny Squat. And furthermore . . . I'll never take another drink with you. It would be beneath me to do so."*

The kind of fate Mr. Flood had in mind is printed here with a small *f;* being a commonplace of life on earth, it is like all other mere facts such as water, money and pipe wrenches. The water leaks from the pipe; the plumber fixes the pipe with his pipe wrench; the owner pays the plumber some money. We can close our eyes to such truths, but we never escape them.

The time, place and other circumstances of our birth, and often of our death, are as far beyond our individual foreknowledge and control as the mating of two giant squids, a thousand feet under the ocean, on the other side of the earth. This particular coupling is no concern of ours; but the facts of our own birth are central to our lives. A word is needed to describe items of such vital significance to us, and over which we have not a shred of control. Little-*f* fate is the word used here.

* From *Old Mr. Flood,* by Joseph Mitchell. Copyright 1943, 1944, 1945, 1948, by Joseph Mitchell. Published by Duell, Sloan and Pearce. Reprinted by permission.

If birth and death are part of our fate, then old Mr. Flood's refusal to drink ever again with the young Alabaman may be taken as part of the latter's big-*F* Fate. Our Fate is that which happens to us because, in some foreseeable way, we have established the conditions or climate in which it is most likely to overtake us.

Contained within the idea of Fate are a host of everyday fallacies about why we are as we are, how we got here, where we are going, and whether we can, or should even try to, change our separate ways of life. To believe that people are no longer susceptible to the old fallacies of Fate and Destiny is sheer delusion. Mankind thrives on fallacy, and we all fool ourselves, all day, every day. We would go mad if we did not.

Has a namby-pamby man with money married a grasping female who runs his life for him, much to his dislike? It is his Fate. Has a professional boxer wound up as a pauper or a physical wreck, or both? It is his Fate. Do more mountain climbers than pianists lose their lives falling over cliffs? It is their Fate.

An unhappily married woman, too modern in her outlook to utter the word fate, may nevertheless conclude that she was fated to meet her future husband at a dance in Ashtabula Falls, and that from that moment she was fated to marry him and fated to unhappiness. Perhaps she thinks the hand of fate works through her husband's character, which is such that she can never be happy with him.

The truth is that *she chanced to meet him, she decided* or *agreed to marry him,* and that, through her words and actions, *she is equally responsible with him* for the unhappiness they share. In placing the blame on fate, she relieves herself of any sense of her own responsibility. Yet we must conclude that the fate she silently blames is best spelled with a big *F;* she is, after all, a cosponsor of her own misery. (In a far more typical and less kindly frame of mind she may, of course, blame only her husband; in such a case he will return the favor, with interest.)

Colloquial synonyms for Fate are 'hard luck,' 'tough luck,' 'the law of averages,' and so on. Such terms also have meanings that are aside from any thoughts of Fate, as when someone loses at poker and we say, "He couldn't beat the law of averages. Tough luck!" To lose at an evening's game of poker is too trivial for anyone but an orangutan to consider it a part of his destiny. On the other hand, the thirty-five-year-old baseball player who can't keep his batting average up is said to be having hard luck; he is a victim of the law of averages. That is to say, *he chose* professional baseball as a career and now, at the age of thirty-five, *he is about to pay the price* of that decision: unemployment. It is his tough luck, all right, and it is also his Fate.

Such Fate may be compounded of mere happenstance, sloppiness, error, or even a reasonably good decision, for which we later refuse to accept responsibility. But to equate this with little-*f* fate is like mistaking a soggy pancake for the sun. Both are round, but the sun is appreciably larger, warmer and more durable. And the sun is hardly ever found in a cold frying pan.

A person's point of view is not, in its entirety, something that the gods have imposed on him or to which he has been fated; for it includes the angle from which he sees things from the precise spot *he chooses* to occupy. Just for example, vocation has much to do with point of view. While in my own adult lifetime I have almost always gained my livelihood within the world of books, I have had many different occupations there. At various times I have been a book editor, a book publisher, a book salesman and a book merchant; now I am a publishers' consultant. So I speak with some authority when I say each of these occupations is very different from each other one, and that special habits of life and a special, characteristic view of books and of life goes with each. In addition, I have at various times in the past had the outlook of a country boy, a college student, a city dweller, a commuter and a father of small children. Though at present I have none of these points of view, I still comprehend them all.

If a man's point of view changes with time, so, too, he may have the power to change it at will, as I pointed out earlier. True, he may *feel* stuck with his angle of view because of some decision made years ago—as in the case of a highly specialized older worker. Generally, though, the man who wants to change his point of view need only change his situation (job, place of residence, et cetera) and, presto! he has a new one. But if he does not wish to lose his grasp of reality, his view had better include the facts of life, among which I include the process of aging and all the other truly universal experiences. He should remember, that is, that his fate is invincible and immutable. But to a degree, and even well beyond the age of fifty, his Fate (with the big F) is still in his own hands.

Is change of point of view advisable? To this question I make no reply; for the only right answer is that which the asker must, in his own wisdom, provide for himself. But enlargement of the field of view is nearly always good. This too can be achieved by an act of will.

Consider the delights of travel. If you want to feast your eyes on different hills and valleys, to hear other languages spoken, to experience a change in climate, to get away from family routines for a while, you can do much worse than take a guided tour of Europe, or such parts of Europe as you have never visited. Your travel agent will handle all the details. If you apply early enough, you need have no worry about tickets, transportation schedules, guides, hotels, restaurants, and what have you. You will travel in a group of garrulous Americans, and you will stop only at those hotels where English is spoken. If you should eat in a restaurant where the waiters speak nothing but Plattdeutsch or Romansh, you can rely on your guide to explain the menu and to place your order. Your laundry will be handled as effortlessly as the sightseeing trips, and absolutely everything will be explained in English. Later on, when you get back home, you can tell all your friends about the wonderful things you saw. And, despite the guides and the crowds of Americans with whom you traveled, you will have broadened your view of the world.

Guided tours are not for me; but right here that is not the point. If you enjoy traveling this way, and if you feel you can get out of it about as much invigoration and uplift as you can stand, then a tour along the lines I have described may be just the ticket. For this is one way to see the monuments of Rome, Fra Angelico's murals in Florence, the Swiss Alps, the boulevards of Paris, the Rembrandts in Amsterdam and The Hague. Far better this way than not at all!

But now suppose that you need more of a change than you could get by seeing the worthy things just mentioned, more than you could get from mere travel, and more than from all these together. Suppose you have done these things, or that for some other reason you know they are not going to give you what you need. What then? Is foreign travel out?

Certainly not. But I suggest that a different kind of travel is in order, and that *the right approach to it is the one that places the fewest barriers between yourself and the people and places you are to visit*. Above all, such travel is an exercise in mindstretching. To see how it can work, let us look in on a couple who have decided to take a trip together.

The first thing they do is to decide where they are going. It so happens that our man, Felix C., had a maternal grandfather who was born in Stockholm. Very good; Stockholm will be one stop. The only foreign language Felix has studied is German; and since he has always been curious about Germany and Austria, it is easily decided to visit Bonn, see the Rhine, and get some of the flavor of life in Vienna, where they will go to the opera. Emma knows a few words of Italian and she shares with Felix an interest in Italian people, art, and cultural history. Fortunately, the C.'s have ample time; they can figure on six weeks in Europe. They arrange to go in the off season, when prices are lower and it is not important to make all reservations in advance.

Felix and Emma prepare their trip with care. He tells his boss what his plans are, and since he works in the textile industry, he asks his employer if there are any European textile machines or processes that should be checked into. It turns out there are two stops Mr. C. can make for his company. One is in Göteborg, Sweden, where one Lars Jensen is said to have developed a new chemical process for the treatment of wool. The other is in Munich, Germany, where a Hans Biedermann claims to have perfected a rival process.

The trip is now four months off, but preparations are already intensive. Felix undertakes to polish up his German, while Emma works on her Italian. To do this they get some challenging conversational courses on phonograph records. They work over their languages almost as if their lives were at stake, because they know that language is the chief barrier between the traveler and the place he is visiting. Every day the records get a working over, and the instructions are closely followed.

Foreign-language books and newspapers are brought into the house. Other books appear in the living room, too, including books on the history, the art, the day-to-day life, and the scenic and other attractions of the four countries where they will stay. Like seasoned European travelers (which they are not), the C.'s also study some large, Swiss-made road maps they found in a bookstore.

One result of all their preparations is that by the time the C.'s arrive in Stockholm they know how they are going to get around, how they are going to live, and what they want to see. They travel second class on the railroads, as most Europeans do. When they arrive at a city where they want to stay, they ask which are the good middle-class hotels. Sometimes, if they do not like the hotel they are in (if, perhaps, there are too many other Americans there), they shop around after a day or two to see if they can find a pleasant *pension*. When they have questions to ask, they ask them almost any-where except at the big travel bureaus that cater to foreign travelers. At mealtimes they stroll around areas where there are restaurants and cafés, and pick one that looks good.

It is not always easy to meet people in a foreign land, even when you travel the way the C.'s do. But there are occasional opportunities, and Felix and Emma rarely miss up on them. In Göteborg and in Munich they are especially lucky, because the chemists that Felix looks up in these cities entertain the C.'s at their homes.

In Göteborg the C.'s are invited to spend an evening with the Jensens, who turn out to be rather formal but extremely pleasant people, whose children ask many questions about America. Like so many other Swedes, the Jensens speak English well. In Stockholm Emma had been struck by the numbers of bouquets and of pushcart vendors selling cut flowers. Now, in the Jensens' apartment, she sees flowers in the foyer, in the living room and in the dining room. In her mind she associates the endless tidy bouquets with the perfect grooming of the beautiful, stylish Swedish women.

Herr Biedermann, in Munich, is soft-spoken and cultured. He takes Felix on a tour of a plant where his process is in use; here Felix learns a great deal about German factory practices, including one thing he is sure his company will want to copy. The chemical process is explained in careful detail, and Herr Biedermann gives Felix some printed matter and a letter on the subject.

The evening is spent at the Biedermann home, where Felix and Emma are fascinated to discover that their host is a Sinologist as well as a chemist. He owns a large collection of Chinese books, many of them superbly illustrated. The walls in the living room are decorated with Chinese prints the likes of which the C.'s have never seen before. Fortunately for

Emma, Mrs. Biedermann speaks a passable English, though Herr Biedermann's is deplorable. Hans finds he can communicate with his host much better in German. The evening passes swiftly as the Biedermanns and the C.'s discuss Chinese art, customs, literature and politics.

In their travels the C.'s find the trains are the best places to strike up conversations with strangers. In a restaurant in Rome a young man asks if he and his wife may sit with the C.'s. They recognize him as a man they had met on the train from Florence. It turns out he is eager to talk with the Americans because the Milanese firm he works for has decided to send somebody to New York as its representative at a trade fair. Naturally, he wants to be chosen. The talk with Emilio lasts for nearly two hours. When they part, the young man has five good reasons why he should be selected to go to New York, and he can't wait to tell them to his boss. The best reason is that Emilio knows that Mr. C. will meet him when he gets there and will introduce him to some people he should know. From the Italian couple the C.'s have learned the names of two fine restaurants to try in Rome, the address of Emilio's parents, in Milan, whom they have promised to visit, and a dozen interesting things they never knew about Italy.

There are other surprises. Mostly, these come about through short conversations carried on in German or Italian. Several of these talks provide delightful insights into matters about which the C.'s had not had the least curiosity. Now that the trip is over, instead of feeling they have just that much less to look forward to, the C.'s are already figuring when they will be able to go abroad again. And in his office Felix has become an expert on European wool technology.

What did Emma and Felix plan to get out of their trip? Certainly not any exciting knowledge of the feeling some Danes have for Sweden or that some north Italians have for Neapolitans. They most certainly did not expect to be enthralled by a seventeenth-century Chinese textbook on art called *The*

Mustard Seed Garden. Yet these very things, and a hundred more, have added greatly to their understanding of the world we live in and to their zest for more knowledge.

Why did the C.'s trip turn out so well? Because they undertook to remove the barriers between themselves and the people in the countries they visited; because they learned the languages as best they could in a short time; because they found their own hotels and *pensions;* because they got their own tickets and made their own decisions as to when to leave one place and go to another; and because they moved around with Europeans instead of at the center of a herd of inwardly terrified American tourists. A German with whom Herr C. struck up a conversation at a railroad station said he was surprised and delighted to discover that Herr C. was an American. "Why, it is impossible!" he said. "Americans never learn to speak German. Surely you must be from Amsterdam, and are joking with me?"

Amazing and wonderful things happen when we open our eyes and ears to the 99.99 per cent of the world about which we know little or nothing.

An inspiring instance of a middle-aged couple who decided to travel and to serve others was reported in *The New York Times* in the spring of 1964. Without further comment, I quote the item here in full, just as it appeared, under the headline, "L.I. Executive, 50, Joins Peace Corps To Work in Africa."

Special to *The New York Times**

FREEPORT, L.I., April 23—David K. Kadane, general counsel to the Long Island Lighting Company, has taken a two-year leave of absence from the company to work in East Africa for the Peace Corps.

He will be sent to Ethiopia, Nyasaland or Tanganyika to assist

* © 1964 by The New York Times Company. Reprinted by permission.

the local governments in establishing legal institutions, drafting codes and laws and training lawyers.

Mr. Kadane, a prominent civic leader in Nassau County, will give up a substantial yearly income to accept the Peace Corps salary of $75 a month plus room and board. He joined the company in 1946 and was named general counsel in 1949.

Mr. Kadane, who is 50 years old, will be joined by his wife, Helene, a nutrition specialist who is a volunteer worker with the United Nations Children's Fund. She will continue her work with the Peace Corps. The couple will start a 10-week training course in June.

Mr. Kadane said that he and his wife had decided to join the Peace Corps because "it's an opportunity to be of service and broaden ourselves. Neither of us has the feeling we are making a sacrifice. We'll get as much as we give."

Travel in North America can be as illuminating as a visit to the Old World; but what we see and hear in our own country may be harder to understand because so many things here are superficially so familiar to us. Here again all depends on the initial approach. You can see America the easy way, by following the beaten paths, seeing only the customary Disneylands and living in your accustomed manner. Your travel agent or your auto club or an airline will be glad to lay it all out for you. On your trip, you will behold some memorable landscapes and eat some good food; but it is unlikely that your mind will be stretched.

The right way, I believe, is to go under your own steam to visit those places in America that strike you as strange or remote, in a geographical or a social sense. I suggest that you dress in comfortable, old clothes, and that if you have two cars, you go in the one that looks the most like an ordinary man's sensible, five-year-old car. In short, try to make yourself invisible.

Have you ever been curious about the American Indian?

Take a trip to South Dakota and set up a base somewhere within an hour's drive of a reservation. Find out what the local people say about the Indians, remembering that while their attitude is important, their facts may be little better than your own. Notice how good or how poor the land is that the Indians have been 'given.'* If you can, make contact with people who live or work on the reservation. If the subject still interests you, go on down to New Mexico or Arizona and do the same there. Learn all you can about opportunities for education and jobs, living standards, the Indians' views of how the government is treating them, and so on. But remember that small talk is the way into conversation with strangers. Nothing much is likely to come of bluntly asking a storekeeper what he thinks of the government's policy on farm price supports.

Having spent a week or two on this project, you will already be a minor expert on the American Indian today. Why do I say such a thing, you ask? Because so few people ever seem to know anything at first hand except their own occupations, their addresses, and the names on their credit cards. The American Indian, being not very numerous and generally hidden away on poor or even worthless land, is little understood by most of us.

A Yankee or a Westerner who does not know the South might do worse than to spend a week or two in some town down that way. If he makes contacts easily, does not waste his time impressing his own views on others, and keeps his eyes open, he will learn a great deal. He will probably discover the charm of some of the South, and he will learn something about the complexity of the relations between the Negroes and the dominant whites.

Being a Yankee, I have never been able to forget something that happened in the early nineteen thirties, on the Eastern

* The land the Indians were 'given' is actually the only part of *their* land that the white man—my forefathers, and perhaps yours—did not steal from them.

Shore of Maryland, where I was a stranger. I was taking my mother for a Sunday drive in the country, on a dirt road, and I remember our car was a three-year-old Ford. We had seen no other car for perhaps five miles and no house for a mile or two when, to our surprise, we suddenly found ourselves driving down the only street of a community of perhaps a dozen small, ramshackle, unpainted houses. At the sight of our car, Negro children who had been playing in the road ran up to the shaded porches. On each porch there were a few chairs, all occupied by adults. Other grownups sat on the steps.

All eyes fixed on us. As these Negroes became aware that a white lady was in the car they all stood up and curtsied politely, smiling warmly as they did so. The men removed their hats and flourished them gracefully in the air, in a way that I thought had been invented by Cecil B. de Mille.

For me this was a weird and shocking experience, because I imagine myself to be the perfect democratic man and cannot conceive that there is any race of people that would bow and scrape in the presence of some other race. But within a few minutes this strange happening began to fit into what I believe is its proper perspective. I recalled that mob lynchings of Negroes still happened there in Queen Annes County, Maryland, at the time. Was not this the reason for all the bowing and hat waving? In any case, the experience has returned to my mind again and again since then, and it has illuminated, in a strange way, my later thoughts about human rights and the inherent dignity and equality of all men.

Travel, as you can see, offers many opportunities for widening our fields of vision. Because travel is so widely advertised and has been made so easy, it is perhaps the most obvious means to the end we seek. Travel that really 'broadens' one, as people used to say, can take us to Europe or keep us in the U.S.A. It can take us to Latin America, to Canada, to Africa, to Asia, or to Polynesia. It can take us to New York City, to St. Louis, to Chicago, to San Francisco, or to Seattle. It may take us only to the next county. Wherever it takes us, we should make contacts with people whose backgrounds and ways of life differ from our own. By doing this, by questioning a little and listening more, by looking carefully, we cannot help but learn much that is new and unexpected. And so we become wiser and more sophisticated, in the best sense of the word. More of life takes on meaning to us and we become more adept at distinguishing between the true and the false, the good and the bad, the light gray and the gray.

If travel broadens us, so can a change of activity right in our home town. Any reader who is interested and who is now, let us say, an executive or a housewife, might try his hand at one of the following occupations, part time or full time, for a few weeks or months: political canvasser, hospital volunteer worker, store clerk, cab driver, census taker, or social worker. But alas! There are few who can qualify for most of these jobs, and those who can may have trouble finding an opening.

Why Not Try
Communication?

THERE ARE THOSE who constantly widen their horizons by reading in various fields, and others who read only in a single field, such as anthropology, science, American history, or medicine. But specialized reading still leaves time for diversity, and there is much to be said for the pursuit of one subject after another.

Some years ago I read T. E. Lawrence's magnificent *Seven Pillars of Wisdom,* a highly personal narrative account of England's desert campaign against the Turks in World War I. Lawrence's book contains a wealth of information about Arabs, the desert, and the way of life there. I followed up my new-found interest in this field by reading *The Hashemite Dynasty,* about a modern family of Middle Eastern kings, and *Arabian Sands,* about an adventure in the Empty Quarter of Arabia; then I read a history of Islam. These four books gave me a little background in Arab life and politics. Now I find that whenever I read a news article about Middle Eastern developments, these recent events fit into a perspective of prior knowledge. Instead of becoming more confused every time something happens in Iraq, I become wiser. Or so I think.

You can use what you already know as a lever to widen your outlook. This may happen through the stimulation provided by a conversation with a friend, a carpenter, a preacher, a psychiatrist, a sea captain, or almost anybody. In holding up your end of the talk, you bring forth certain relevant items of experience and thought. Just the mental exercise of doing this can shed light into some dark corner. But in true conversation something else is added, by which I mean the comments and counterideas of the person you are talking with. Great, almost blinding insights have been provided through such exchanges.

But alas! There are exceedingly few good listeners in this world; and no conversation worthy of the name can be conducted with a person who will not listen. The fact that someone is silent while you are talking is not a sign that he is listening; as a rule it shows only a polite (or grudging) recognition that it is your turn to talk. If both parties want to converse, then each will respond with an answer that at least includes an implied acknowledgment of what the other has just said. Otherwise the talk is mere chat, like a chattering of monkeys. And it is probably duller than monkey talk.

Correspondence has certain points in common with conversation; it has its disadvantages and its advantages. It calls for an exchange of views, but is less spontaneous and generally less gay. Being a more considered exercise, it covers its ground less rapidly but can do so more thoroughly than conversation, when desired. One of the advantages of correspondence is that one's friends often live far away. The telephone, good as it is for exchanging greetings and making dates, will hardly do.

Letter writing takes different forms. Letters are written to complete strangers and to lovers; they may be written to persuade or to influence others; they are written to explain away misunderstandings; some letters request advice; others are written to amuse; many convey news. Letters may be designed to keep old friendships warm or to break them off, to enter a plea or to offer thanks or an apology. Many letters are simply acknowledgments.

He who has the time and the energy can scarcely write too many letters, provided their quality is good. People have always enjoyed receiving mail; the kind they like most, after envelopes containing money, is often the spontaneous letter from a friend. Correspondence with acquaintances is more limited than correspondence with friends. One may ask an acquaintance for help in selecting a hotel, or ask almost any question he might be expected to answer. Favors may be offered and asked, news of special interest may be volunteered, and so forth.

Correspondence with friends offers unique opportunities for congenial communication. Friends may be exposed to things that would scare the daylights out of acquaintances, for true friendship is commonly based on more knowledge, each person of the other, than would be tolerable to mere acquaintances.

The more serious letters to a friend may communicate some thoughts on larger matters, some ideas, some hopes, some tentative plans for the future in the expectation that such disclosures will stimulate the friend to send an interesting reply. I do not say that news should be excluded; on the contrary, I hold that news, like the lead paragraph in a newspaper article, is often the strong peg on which the rest of a letter hangs. If not the peg, in a logical sense, it may nonetheless be the excuse for the letter.

Like much would-be conversation, which is mere noise, letters are often ruined by a clutter of trivia. My mild advice is to omit from letters to friends all the truly undignified, mean, dull things which already take up so much of our lives, leaving always too little of life for that which is meaningful or interesting or enjoyable.

Personal letters cannot be written by prescription, for a letter to a friend not only must be in the style of the writer, but also will reflect his life and interests. So it is that even I must regard my suggestions, above, merely as guideposts to be followed or ignored—more likely the latter.

To illustrate the principle that the best of letters have a character all their own, often in defiance of any rules, I have chosen to reprint here a letter written by Bartolomeo

Vanzetti while in a Massachusetts prison with Niccolo Sacco for allegedly participating in a holdup and murder. Both men were later convicted and executed, though many have steadfastly believed them innocent. Recent re-examination of the evidence has led to a more general acceptance of the verdict of guilt, at least for Sacco; I do not presume to any knowledge of their guilt or innocence.

Vanzetti, an anarchist, came to the United States from Italy in 1908, at the age of twenty. Here he worked as a laborer and a fish peddler. He and Sacco were arrested for murder in May, 1920. After various trials and appeals, the two were executed shortly after midnight, August 22, 1927. So, Vanzetti was in prison for over seven years. While there he worked in the prison paint shop and then as a tailor. He was regarded as a model prisoner. He read a great deal and wrote many letters in Italian and English; his command of English was poor at first, but it improved with the years in prison. Vanzetti had a rare gift of self-expression.

The letter* I have chosen was written to one of the many who believed Vanzetti innocent and who gave him moral support after his arrest.

1921, CHARLESTOWN STATE PRISON

MY DEAR MRS. EVANS:†

The "wake up" rings here in Charlestown at 7 A.M. but yesterday morning, the officer call me at six o'clock. "Go to put on your own clothes," he tell me with hurried way. I went and I found my old clothing horribly wrinkled. There were nobody at the work, at such hour, so, after a useless protest I was compelled to put them on as they were. Well, I was saying to myself, returning to the cell: There is, after all, something worse than this.

---

† Mrs. Elizabeth Glendower Evans, of Brookline, Mass.

Sure it was: On the table I found my breakfast, a cup of coffee, three slices of bread, two frankforts and mashed potatoes, all so cold as ice cream can be.

After such a breakfast, an official took me in the "Guard Room." The little chauffeur, an old officer, and the bravest one were waiting for me. I was chained with the last one, and all four left the room and went down to the street where the automobile was ready. Six or seven officers stood at the door, with their right hand near the back pocket, ready to protect me from any attack. One must be most ungrateful man of the world for not feeling quite reconoscent.

As the machine start I asked for tobacco. They stop at the nearest corner and the old officer went to buy some of it. A young policeman begin to speak with the remaining officers, he leaning himself in such a manner to put his head in the automobile. His eyes, dark and clear, look at me with an ill-concealed curiosity, and I perceive his wonder at my common harmless presence. Surely he had expected something different. Meanwhile I was looking at the people going up and down of the streets. I can tell which of them are employed and which are not by their way of walking.

The former went straight ahead as men who know where he want to go and when he must arrive. The second look around, above and below, as a man who lost himself, and do not know what he has to do. Little farther I meet a little compatriot. He is a little fellow of the South, with yellow pale face dry by a copious dayly sweat, but his mustachs are well curled up. He is very petty, and it look like if he were the centre of the world. I cannot help but smile. I never see him before but I know where he go, what he thinks; his hopes. I knew him, as I know myself; probably better than myself. "Take that way; avoid civilization," the brave officer is now crying to the driver who obey silently. Surely enough this man hope that such high language is incomprehensible to me.

So we enter now into a Park the name of which I already forget, but the beauty of it, I will never forget anymore. If I were poet and know the metre, I would write a song of it in third rhyme. I am not a poet, but neither so profane to disturb such splendor with my poor ink. The concerned officer point to me a big brick building, saying, "It is the Fine Arts Museum." He point many other buildings saying that they are almost all a private schools. I was then regretting to have only a pair of eyes, able to look in one direction alone. I observe everything, the trees, the bushes, the grass, the rocks, and the brook along the way, on which I was raptured. The drops of dew look like pearls; the sky reflects himself in the waters of the brook, and let one think that it is bottomless. But beauty over all tell to me a wonderful history of one day, far away, a day when the waters in a gigantic and confounded waves, left this place suddenly.

I look now to those which pass at my side in automobiles. But what a difference between these men that I meet now, and those I met a little while ago, a little far away going to work, or walking round about; what a difference! The big buildings had now give the place to a more modest ones, which become more and more rare, until only a little, humble, odd, funny houses, rise here and there from the accidentated soil. O, funny, humble, old, little houses that I love; little house always big enough for the greatest loves, and most saint affections. Here I see two girls of the people going to work. They look like to be sisters. Their shoulders are more large than those of the girls I meet a little before, but little curved. On their pale faces are lines of sorrow and distress. There is sobberness and suffering in their big, deep, full eyes. Poor plebian girls, where are the roses of your springtime?

I found myself in front of Dedham jail. We enter. A little ugly Napolitan barber has such a care and zeal of my looking, as if I am the Mayor of Naple.

They locked me at No. 61. Now the news of my arrival is known by all the human canaries of the place. The poor boys do their best to give me a glance, a word, a cheer up. Little after I was brought to the Court, protected by a numerous American Cossack, as if I and Nick were a Russian Czars.

At last we come back to Charlestown, and I have had the opportunity to look at the sky and see the stars, as in the old days at home. The workers were then coming back home. Still in their confused forms I can see the "little of abdom and much of heart" as Gori sang. One of them appear to be a Latin, strong and noble. This is one of those who will win the battle that the citizens had lost, I say to myself.

Few minutes after we stop in front of the Prison, and little after I found myself carefully closed in my room, where a supper, something like tea and coffee, boiled beef and mashed potatoes with few slices of bread, wait for me, all as cold as ice cream can be.

For some, the suggestion that they enter into correspondence with a friend will raise formidable obstacles. There are those, possibly, who have no friends whatever; and how many have a friend capable of anything better than back-fence gossip? Many a reader, also, will doubt his ability as a writer, or will fear that his letters may betray some inner weakness or failing. Why? Surely he has feelings, ideas, and news worth imparting to an old and trusted friend?

Certain psychological obstacles to thoughtful letter writing shed light on an unfortunate quirk of American society. Too often we fear to say anything profound or moving, lest in doing so we give away some awful secret. Why, in the name of God, should this be? What secrets do we have that must be kept at such cost? What power do we attribute to others, that we dread their judgment? Do we fear that, given the truth at last, our friends will burn us in effigy? Are we cowards, living in perpetual terror of nothing more than what others might think? Have we no fair regard for ourselves?

If we are merely shallow and ignorant, or if we have profound or moving things to say, let us now, past the mid-point of our lives, expose the truth at last to a chosen friend or two;

for so much the sooner will they come to know us as we are, and so be able to renew their friendship with us or turn from us, be they false friends only.

There is a force in our society which breeds our fear of honest communication; but, as I will show, this is a fear of shadows only. At the age of fifty we can safely classify these shadows with the ogre that lived in the closet, when we were very young. The ogre is amusing in retrospect; but today its most impressive characteristic is its lack of reality. If, at our age, things that are so patently unreal dominate not only our thoughts, but our communications and our actions as well, then it is time to do something about ourselves.

What, then, is the force that seeks to prevent us from writing the truth to a friend?

It is the force of a defective democratic education that has taught us the advantages of agreeing with everybody else, of living and thinking in groups and as groups. Failing in this, we have been led to believe, we must live out our days as loners or pariahs. Out of education for group-think comes the desire to be universally liked, because we have concluded that we will get out of touch and drift into non-group-think if the group does not like us. Then, too, we believe we can be liked only if we share equally in the group, or inherently human, characteristics. Note that being human is being *the same* as other humans, a thought which suggests that all people, being precisely hundred-per-cent human, must be equally likable.

Not quite. There is also assumed to be a fragile, indefinable difference between all likable and genuinely human people. It is this gossamer (or even false) individuality we fear the truth may destroy, thereby reducing us to the lowest common denominator. If this terrible thing should happen, we would stand revealed in our spiritual nakedness, lonely, starved for love, neglected, without recourse. And sometimes it is the 'myth' of our humanity we fear the truth will destroy; for we sense that under the skin we are only a kind of animal.

So now the picture starts to emerge. We fear that if we say something 'wrong' in a letter, we may reveal ourselves as shallow and ignorant, or even brutal, and hence lacking in that indefinable, fragile quality that our friend supposed to be uniquely ours, or we may show ourselves as people who have broken with the group and are plunging downward on some Godforsaken and unutterably lonely course. One way or another we will have labeled ourselves as outsiders, losers, or both at once.

Neither the overweening desire to be liked by all, for our common humanity, nor the illusion that we are individually likable for some immensely perishable, unique quality is a necessary adjunct to our democratic form of government. Yet the heartsick wish for general approbation is the cause of much misdirected effort and futile soul searching. To the extent that we can kill this wish in ourselves, we are liberated from a tyranny, and at no cost.

So, if you have the crippling point of view of one who craves the admiration and love of all, I invite you to rise and move a few rows further back in the stadium. Note that from back here you can easily see that the other spectators are not looking toward where you were just sitting, as you may have thought they were. Mostly they are just straightening their ties, tidying their hair, looking at their fingernails, and nervously wondering what everybody else is thinking about *them*. They are wasting their time, the way you were wasting yours when you thought they were looking at you.

Correspondence is a process of illumination. The writer, like the reader, is obliged to stand back of the light, to see that which is illuminated; and in so shifting his position he acquires a wider and better view. If there is somebody to receive your letter and to reply to it, do not let any shapeless fears deny you the privilege of writing it properly and sending it off.

Letter writing, travel, reading—these can all be used to broaden, to deepen and to sharpen our view of things. But this is only a minute sample of the immense variety of steps that can be taken to achieve the same ends. Intensive studies in such fields as nature, psychology, paleontology, chemistry, physics, history, mathematics, the theater, biography and anatomy are some other adventures that cannot help but widen our horizons and give our lives more meaning.

The world is full of adventures that await him who will have them. Right now is a good time to begin tracking them down.

Friendship

THE BEST OF LIFE is celebration, and we need only open our eyes to find things without end to revel in. We can celebrate our wives and husbands, the tasty food we eat, the tight roofs over our heads, the warm coats that keep out the winter wind, the tingle and warmth of slick liquor going smoothly down. We can justifiably celebrate the size of corporate dividends when they come our way, we can enjoy the security of civil-service jobs or the larger salaries of more hazardous employment, and we can shout from the roof tops the delights of carefree retirement and careless love. Above all we can and should celebrate that we, only we of all that ever were, are still living.

It was Robert Louis Stevenson who said, "There is no duty we so much underrate as the duty of being happy." There is much truth in this; how much, we can barely guess from the many people we all know who live by cursing their jobs, their wives, their husbands, their children, the weather, and the politicians and government that stand between themselves and anarchy or tyranny. How many waste good liquor by drinking it only to forget lives that should make them happy or lives which they should change if they do not! Most of us are luckier than we know, and have much to celebrate.

But happiness and joyful celebration are inconceivable without friends, and it is awful to imagine the loneliness of otherwise fortunate people who have no friends anywhere. Their plight should give us pause, because most of us find that, through neglect, the number of our own friends has declined with the years. So, at fifty, the condition of our friendships may need more attention than it did long ago, when we were very young and friends were made quickly and easily. We should hold on to old friends when we can; we should replace them when necessary. This is more easily said than done, but better done than undone.

The virtues of automobiles, soap and cigarettes are widely proclaimed as I write these words; but who will launch an advertising campaign on behalf of friendship? In other times the most educated men thought and wrote freely about it, because they understood that friends could make a man happy and that a friendless life could be worse than a childless marriage. The Greeks and the Romans knew quite a bit about the subject and, realizing its importance, tried to learn more. Aristotle, in his *Ethics,* inquired into the matter, and Cicero wrote about it in his essay "On Friendship." In the Apocryphal Book of Ecclesiasticus it is written that "A friend is the medicine of life." The Elizabethan poet Nicholas Breton classifies the curse of friendlessness with that of poverty in the lines,

> *I wish my deadly foe no worse*
> *Than want of friends, and empty purse.*

In the nineteenth century Ralph Waldo Emerson said a friend was "a person with whom I may be sincere. Before him I may think aloud." In "A Week on the Concord and the Merrimack Rivers" Thoreau wrote that friends "cherish each other's hopes. They are kind to each other's dreams." He also said, "Friendship is never established as an understood relation. . . . It is a miracle which requires constant proofs. It is an exercise of the purest imagination and of the rarest faith."

The splendid title of David Riesman's book *The Lonely Crowd* is foreshadowed by a sentence in Francis Bacon's essay "Of Friendship," published 366 years ago. "A crowd is not company," wrote Bacon, "and faces are but a gallery of pictures."

Close friendships may never have been so scarce as they are today, when people are more numerous than ever. The rarity of warm friendships and what should be done about it are matters that cry for the attention of good general thinkers; but nothing happens, because ours is not an age in which a general thinker has much chance of making a living. The supply of such intellects is about equal to the demand, which, as I look through the extensive "Help Wanted" columns of today's *New York Times,* appears to be exactly zero.

If there are no jobs for general thinkers, there are plenty for specialists. There are lots of openings for engineers, cost accountants, efficiency experts, and oceanographers, and for most jobs there are at least a few qualified applicants. Few specialists, on the other hand, concern themselves with friendship, because there is no money in it. There are some ministers and rabbis who can talk usefully about the subject; F.B.I. agents look into a person's friendships when they seek to measure his loyalty to the United States government. Among psychiatrists there are a few clear thinkers capable of shedding light on the dynamics of friendship; but, like other specialists, psychiatrists write mostly for each other.

Who can speak about friendship, clearly and with feeling, to the person lost in the press of the lonely crowd? Who can explain to him, so that he will listen, that a friend is the medicine of life? Who will elucidate for him, as he heads into Times Square on New Year's Eve, that a crowd is not company?

Aristotle seems to have been the best student of friendship; what he said about it in Athens twenty-three centuries ago can still be studied with profit. That philosopher discovered three kinds of friendship worthy of the name. Each one is good for us and adds to our happiness, and there can be several degrees of each kind. The first is based on utility; an example would be a friendship between people who do business together. The second has its roots in a quest for pleasure; it can be seen in the case of friendship between amusing or quick-witted persons. The third is the best; in it each friend seeks nothing beyond the company and the happiness of the other. Most poets who write about friendship mean only Aristotle's third and best kind, while in everyday speech we commonly refer to all three types as if they were the same. In fact, we often erroneously speak of mere acquaintances as friends.

The most perishable, and those fullest of complaint, are the friendships of utility or business, in which each party seeks something useful to himself; the salesman wants to sell, and his customer wants to buy cheaply. If either party moves to another line of business, the friendship will be all over, because the two people will no longer be able to swap the practical favors which the friendship demanded.

Less perishable and more pleasant, says Aristotle, are the friendships between witty people. So long as the people themselves do not change, as by becoming dull or sour, they may continue to amuse each other and so remain good friends.

Friendships based on utility and those based on wit are essentially selfish. Each friend wants to get something out of the other. In one case he wants something useful *for himself;* in the other he wants amusement *for himself.* The emphasis is always on oneself, not on the other party to the friendship.

But selflessness is the rule in the best of friendships. What benefits my friend, benefits me; what benefits me, benefits him. This is so, not because we share our worldly goods with each other (we don't), but because, being true friends, we take pleasure in each other's good fortune. It is true that people who are friends in the deepest sense do favors for each other; but these favors, whether large or small, are an incidental part of the friendship and are not essential to its prosperity. Such favors ought not to be confused with the many tokens of friendship, such as invitations to dinner and the exchange of gifts.

While friendships of mere utility are most prone to argument and are the most easily dissolved, those friendships that lack any selfish motive are unlikely to be marred by argument and are the most durable. In ideal friendship, there being no personal ends to gain, there is no reason for heated argument; Aristotle says that if a difference of opinion should arise, the good friend takes his revenge by doing well by the other.

A deeply loved mate may grow into a close friend, especially in old age, but as a rule wives and husbands, no matter how happy together, can scarcely be thought of as friends. This does not imply that love is inferior to friendship, but only that it is different. If married love is nevertheless to be regarded as a form of friendship, then it must be seen as a friendship based on utility or pleasure. For there is a kind of happy barter in any happy marriage; the more joyfully one gives, the more ecstatically the other receives. But if either party withholds his or her sexual favors, and transfers them to another, the friendship will be at an end.

It was Francis Bacon who wrote most clearly about the importance of friendship. Unlike Aristotle, he did not distinguish between the three kinds; he was interested only in true friendship, the third and best variety. Bacon said:

No receipt openeth the heart but a true friend, to whom you may impart griefs, joys, fears, hopes, suspicions, counsels, and whatsoever lieth upon the heart to oppress it, in a kind of civil shrift or confession. . . .

This communicating of a man's self to his friend works two contrary effects, for it redoubleth joys and cutteth griefs in halves; for there is no man that imparteth his joys to a friend, but he joyeth the more; and no man that imparteth his griefs to a friend, but he grieveth the less.

Another fruit of friendship is illuminated by a tale told me about the poet Mark Van Doren, one of the valued teachers I had at Columbia. He had sat silently through a long discussion between two other men; then one of the talkers turned to him and said, "What do you think about this, Mark?"

"How can I tell what I think," Van Doren replied, "when I haven't said anything yet? You two have been doing all the talking."

A true friend is a person we can talk to freely and easily. The private talk of two friends helps both to learn what they really think about the subject of conversation. Even when they know what they think, comfortable talk between friends improves the ideas of both. A man who reveals his thoughts to a friend, said Bacon, "waxeth wiser then himself; and that more by an hour's discourse than by a day's meditation."

A friend can advise us alike about personal matters and about business affairs; we may not follow his advice, but we need never worry that he will be offended if we do not do as he suggests. A friend may see our problem better than we do, because he is detached from our worried, personal involvement in it, while we see it only in bits and pieces, with our minds and with our bellies. His advice may therefore be better than any we could offer ourselves.

A friend is, in a sense, an extension of one's self. There are occasions in life when a person needs somebody to plead his case. A friend can and will do this; he can even make extravagant claims without the embarrassment we would feel if we had to make the case ourselves. It is also true that things that are incomplete on one's death will be seen to by a friend.

It is pleasant to visit with a friend; it is even pleasant simply to know that he exists. Somehow that knowledge improves the world immensely, making it at once a warmer and more secure place in which to live.

There is a modern testimony to friendship in the book *Emotional Problems of Living,* by the psychiatrists Dr. O.

Spurgeon English and Dr. G. H. J. Pearson. At one point these men say:

> Children need to be noticed and thought about and talked about in order to gain a comfortable healthy feeling of self-esteem. Grownups need the same thing. Friends give this to each other by talking about shared ideas, feelings, and experiences. Friends are more than a luxury—they are a necessity. They are important not for *what they can give us,* but because of what inevitably comes back when *we give ourselves to them.**

This brings to mind two lines from Walt Whitman's poem "Song of Myself":

> *Behold I do not give lectures or a little charity,*
> *When I give I give myself.*

Dr. Samuel Johnson said that a person should keep his friendships in constant repair, and should make new acquaintances as he advances through life. Certainly if friendships are good, neglect of friends is bad. To keep friendships in good repair calls for patience, an output of energy, an expenditure of time, and even, sometimes, an outlay of money. A person who allows his friendships to decay is little better than one who neglects his clothing or his roof; he reminds me of the man who was visited by the Arkansas Traveler. According to one version of the tale, the traveling man stopped one day for shelter at a one-room shack inhabited by a lazy woodsman and his wife. "Why don't you fix the roof?" asked the salesman. "Caint," said the woodsman. "It's raining."

Some time later the traveler stopped by on a clear day. "Now that it has cleared off, why don't you fix that hole in the roof?" he inquired. "Why bother?" his host said. "Taint raining."

As we celebrate life, we need always to prepare for more celebration. Part of this preparation is the making of new acquaintances in the hope that, through cultivation, some will become tomorrow's friends. The person who always has friends about has much to celebrate and ample opportunity to do so. An evening with one or more friends can be a joyous event; but it was Bacon, remember, who said that a crowd is not company. A party with no friends there, but only a lot of nodding acquaintances, can be a lonely affair.

Anybody with a lively interest in the present and in the future, anybody whose disposition makes him worth having as a friend, can make friends at any age. Dr. Flanders Dunbar's study of hundreds of centenarians shows that such very old people often have many friends. It should be obvious that nearly all those friends are made in later life, mostly after the age of seventy.

We lose friends by death, migration and neglect; we win new friends by mingling and by being outgoing. Volumes could be written on the subject of winning friends, but I find it hard to improve on two lines by Walt Whitman:

Stranger, if you passing meet me and desire to speak to me,
why should you not speak to me?
And why should I not speak to you?

Try This
for the Next Half Century
(Then, If It Doesn't Work,
Try Something Else)

WHAT FURTHER WORDS can I use to stress sufficiently the importance of healthy reflection, of activity and of laughter, to the person who is going on from fifty to an age which he can enjoy more than any other, and in which he can love and be loved more than in any other? I have tried many different ways in these pages, and I will try others in the hope that each extra argument to the point may light the way for a few more people.

We get out of life what we put into it, a little more or a little less. Complaints may be returned as nagging, with interest; excessive idleness often pays off in fear and nervousness, in boredom and loneliness. Too much physical activity may endanger our health or take us to a dead end where we find ourselves in foolish competition with our muscle-bound juniors.

But reflection which we undertake with purpose and with hope mirrors us as we are and as we should like to be. It shows us our limitations and our capabilities. It tells us what we want out of life, and how much of what we want we may sensibly seek. Even idle reflection has been known to pay off with marvelous insights and inspirations.

Do not confuse reflection with daydreaming. One shows us the shape of life, as it is and as we might make it. The other, peopled with caricatures, is only a comic-strip flight from reality.

God or our monkey ancestors, or both, gave us our muscled legs, arms, fingers and backs; these are superbly designed for action. The brain is the chief executive and administrator in charge of this equipment. Through laziness or a misunderstanding of its task, the brain may fail to direct the body to act as purposefully or as intensively as it should. Then we grow rusty, and brain and body decline together. But action, especially when it is well directed, polishes, ennobles and refines us. This is true whether the action is of a breadwinning sort, whether it is housework, whether it is social work, or whether it is creative effort. Action toward a preconceived end soon acquires a driving power of its own. A little thought may have been needed to set it going in the right direction, but soon the activity seems to become a purpose in itself and colors our life with meaning.

Laughter is a way of life. The high priests of laughter, like the high priests of anything, dominate the congregations of the true believers. Laughter helps us to see the good in mean little people, and the picayune in the great. It brings us joy as we look in the mirror, early in the morning, with our eyes half closed, our hair on end, our jowls unshaven, or—if we are female—with our make-up missing. Easy, uncomplicated laughter helps us to embrace hard truths quickly, as we should. Almost any laughter is easier than weeping, which for most adults seems virtually impossible; laughter is less embarrassing, too, and more enjoyable—not quite, but almost always.

Those who live longest and are happiest are laughers and doers. Alas, there are no statistics to tell us whether these long-lived people are also reflective. Reflect on that, if you will, and if it makes you laugh, do something about it.

Revenge at Last!

ONE OF HOLLYWOOD's all-time funniest comedians was Edgar Kennedy, a balding, florid man who could bring down the house merely by standing motionless while other comics ripped off his tie, dented the fenders of his car, demolished his house, embraced his wife, and threw pies in his face. But unlike Buster Keaton, with whom he sometimes appeared, Kennedy was no meekling. On the contrary, he played the part of a big, strong, silent man with high blood pressure and a vile temper who, by Herculean effort, was barely able to keep from running amok in response to the indignities others heaped on his head. The longer he held himself back, the funnier he was, and I am sure I was not the only Kennedy fan who feared the comedian would burst a blood vessel if he did not quickly let off steam.

In the end he would return tit for tat; but while his adversaries struck quickly and compulsively, Kennedy's actions, like his heroic self-restraint, were always deliberate. He had a trick of picking up a custard pie in a slow, studied manner. Then, instead of throwing it, he would push it firmly against his tormentor's face, and hold it there.

Entire comedies were stuffed tight with assaults on Kennedy's dignity. Buster Keaton, perhaps, would ask him to hold a nail while he hammered it in. Keaton would miss and hit Kennedy's finger. Then we would see our hero carrying a bowl of soup in a cafeteria. An overdressed woman would bump into him and spill the soup down the front of his new suit. A fly would land on Kennedy's nose; somebody would swat it. So he would plod on, from disaster to disaster, becoming more and more furious, but still not striking back. You wondered which would happen first: Would Kennedy take his vengeance, as he had every right to do, or would he simply explode? The suspense was unbearable.

Keaton was sometimes a nearly opposite type. While Kennedy restrained himself for fear of the tremendous damage he might do if unleashed, Keaton would hold back because he was afraid of what others might do to him. A favorite Keaton predicament was one in which he would be about to get even for some rank injustice when, in the nick of time, he would get his first good look at his tormentor, a huge ogre of a man who could crush Keaton between thumb and forefinger. Sometimes, when things got very rough, Keaton would cry from pain or mere frustration. But in the end—and usually before that—the little man would strike back.

It is a good thing people do not often get put upon the way Kennedy and Keaton were. As things are, of course, the causes of offense in our real world are more than sufficiently numerous, though most of the indignities we suffer are less personal than having somebody step on our corns. Today the author of the offense is usually some faceless government office or corporation.

One of life's great pleasures, and sometimes one of the necessities of life, is striking back against those who strike at us, particularly after we have turned our cheek again and again, and have been slapped each time. Fifty years being about long enough for anybody to play at cheek turning, I urge those who have been restraining themselves all these years to make up their minds that, with the human comedy half over, it's high time they took charge. Letting off steam is a very healthful experience, and it's often heaps of fun.

A good first step is to make a list of things that annoy you.

Here, off the top of my head, are a few items that have gotten under my skin:

ENTERTAINMENT:

Actors who can't act

Comedians who are merely offensive—if that

Interruption of TV commercials by programs (I hold the commercials are the best part)

All spectacular movies (except *Lawrence of Arabia*)

All musical comedies on film

Newsreels that give me ten seconds of this, and three seconds of the other—when what I want is a few minutes for each item

Newsreel fashion shows

'Frank' and 'adult' movies (I'm not opposed to nudity and sex in movies—only to the corny commercial uses of them)

AUTOMOBILES:

Tail fins

Double headlights and double tail lights (two on each side)

New models every year

Cars that look like pregnant hippopotami on their way to the delivery room

'Sleek lines' and the 'Continental look'—which only mean the car is too long for today's crowded streets

DRIVERS:

The heel who won't dim or lower his bright lights as he approaches me

The clod who zips out of his driveway onto the road ahead of me, then slows to fifteen miles an hour, carefully holding the center of the road as he does so

The hare-brained female who is so busy talking to her pal she forgets she is driving

The mother who parks at an intersection, usually in the center of it, while her youngster waits for the school bus

OTHER PEOPLE:

Fund raisers who put me to shame by giving me the names of

friends who have given more than I intend to or can. (My response: I don't give anything; or if it's an educational cause about which I'm enthusiastic, I may give through some other channel.)

All other holdup men, whether armed or not

Store clerks who size me up

People who throw their weight around

People who ask questions, but never listen to answers

Tyrants—whether at the head of government or family

People who don't know their own business

MISCELLANEOUS:

All-electric homes, wired for total failure when the wires go down or disaster strikes

Bad reporting in newspapers

Newspapers that don't print the news, and newspapers that freely inject editorial opinion into their headlines and news stories

Overuse of DDT, dieldrin, and all dangerous insecticides and weed killers that are needlessly killing off wildflowers, fish, game, earthworms, and songbirds—and uglifying the landscape

Poor workmanship in anything whatever

This is not the place to list all the different types of vengeance that can be taken against people, things and faceless organizations that torment us. There isn't room for that; a few suggestions must suffice. The best counterstrokes, of course, are those that stand some chance of diminishing the evil, or at least of protecting us from it.

Not long ago, S. I. Hayakawa, the famous American semanticist, who lives in California, found a satisfactory way of striking back at his local telephone company when, to his annoyance, that firm announced it was going to put in all-digit dialing. Hayakawa and others who rallied around him preferred the traditional centrals, the names of which provide the two-letter prefixes to phone numbers. These men banded together to get what they wanted, and that is how the famous Anti-Digit-Dialing League was formed. So far as I know, the League has had no important success to date; but it has won nationwide support, it has demonstrated that the all-number system is unnecessary to national dialing, and it has even brought at least one lawsuit against a phone company. Even if the League wins no victories, it has served a useful purpose by showing people how to band together to fight for what they want. And if others refuse to learn from his example, Hayakawa can always take comfort in the knowledge that his crusade was good fun.

Life is too short for us all to set up or even to join societies that are opposed to this, that and the other. But a little bit of such activity on everybody's part can go a long way toward making business and government more responsive to our needs.

Does a store you patronize displease you? Let the owner or manager know why; then, if the condition is not corrected, take your trade elsewhere.

Has some division of your city or state government given you poor service or abused you in any way? Write to the mayor or the governor, telling him all about it. You'll be surprised to find how much good this can do. (Several years ago I addressed a routine letter about a tax refund to the New York State Tax Commission. No answer came, so I sent one follow-up, then another. After nearly a year without an answer I addressed a complaint to the then governor, W. Averell Harriman. In short order I had an acknowledgment, a favorable decision and a check.)

Do you think the Social Security law should be improved? Tell your Senators, your Congressman and the President just what to do.

Does some political aspirant, who just might be elected to high office, strike you as a low-grade comic or an incompetent? Write a short, pointed letter to a newspaper. (*The New York Times* recently ran a letter that claimed one politician "opens his mouth only to change feet.")

Although youth may not be grateful for the fact, and I don't think it should be, there is little reason to dispute those sociologists who contend that America is a child-and-youth-centered nation. In *The House of Intellect,* Jacques Barzun says, "Americans began by loving youth, and now, out of adult self-pity, they worship it."

But if Americans worship youth, American business idolizes it, often in defiance of the most elementary economics. An ever-ready illustration of this idolatry is the vast amount of TV and magazine advertising that business directs at the young. Of course, the easiest people to sell to are those with ample free cash. People under thirty and those over fifty have one thing in common here; on the average they are less encumbered with family and installment obligations than are those from thirty through forty-nine. Insofar as they have substantial incomes, both groups are relatively free to respond favorably to the blandishments of the big advertisers.

So far, so good; but how about income? With the single exception of the fully retired, the youngest group harbors the largest numbers of the small earners and the nonearners. Here are the millions still pursuing their education; the millions in the armed services; the millions of unemployed and only semi-employed among the unskilled; the other millions on the bottom rung of the promotion ladder. Shifting our focus now from the lowest incomes to the highest, we find that for each person under thirty who had an income of $10,000 or more in 1960, there were eleven persons in their forties with such incomes, and thirteen aged fifty and more.

As against the argument of purchasing power—which you might think would be the only argument of interest to business—consider now the evidence of the consumer advertising of the big manufacturers.

A study I made of advertising in magazines of mass circulation in 1962 showed five times as many ads slanted to the under-thirty as to all those aged forty and more. This despite the fact that the forty-plus accounted for twenty-four times as many of the good incomes as did the twenty-nine-minus!

Does American business worship youth—or, as I said earlier, isn't "idolize" the correct word?*

Elsewhere I say that, after fifty, people tend to become more self-centered. This tendency is commonly accentuated later on, and some students of gerontology hold that disengagement from the world around us is one of the hallmarks of true old age. Mostly, these students do not argue that such disengagement is a bad thing; they merely observe it as a fact.

It seems likely that the disengagement of the old is more pronounced in the United States than in countries where old age is held in higher esteem. This should not seem strange in view of the extent to which American society, and especially business, caters to the young. If 'youth will be served,' what does it matter what the fifty-plus want?

It is interesting to think of one's acquaintances among the middle-aged and the late-middle-aged, one by one, in an effort to discover how each reacts to our youth-slanted society. A few, at least, try to adopt the tastes, the manners, the customs, and even the thoughts of the youngest adult group. Such a response to commercial youth-idolatry demands a nearly impossible acting out of a fantasy of youthfulness. To imitate a younger generation—particularly the all-false younger generation pictured in the advertisements—one must reject one's

* I know the arguments for selling to youth, but this is not the place to state them. Good as some of them are, furthermore, they are not nearly good enough to justify the present extent of the youth-bias in advertising.

own tastes, training and identity. This, of course, is precisely what the advertisers want. They seek to manipulate the preferences of the more gullible young in the expectation that the latter will in turn manipulate our preferences. The advertisers lead the youth, and the youth leads us—too often.

When I was a boy there lived in the town of Dover, New Jersey, an unmarried woman whose age I was too young to judge. To me, a child of ten when I became aware of her, she seemed old. In fact, she may have been thirty. Tilly fancied herself a young thing of sixteen. Her acting out of her fantasy provided a touching caricature of any woman trying to look younger than her years. What made her striking was that on Sundays she wore a girl's Easter clothes of a style that had gone out years earlier. Her dress was long, billowing and gay; on her head she wore a flower garden. To a crude boy she was hilariously funny.

I include the sketch of Tilly only because it points to the supreme irony of the youth fantasy, which is that acting it out may strike some people as nothing but an act after all. So, unless the object is laughter, why bother?

A different response to a youth-centered America is to rebel against it by rejecting everything that is new or that smacks of youth. A person who so reacts feels compelled to reject new fads and products as they come along, not on their merits, but just because they are new and he associates them with the values of youth. To respond in this way, a man or a woman must be cussedly proud of his age. Yet a certain pride of age is needed in America today.

The youth-talk of the advertisers and the special tastes of the self-centered young are not designed to make the older American disengage himself from society; the mere denial of the possibility at once shows how ridiculous the idea is. The advertiser, to put it kindly, is just a bit dense. He desperately wants to sell to everybody and, as he might put it, "especially you." Despite its craving for independence and a life of its own, youth sincerely wants its parents to go on living and to go on enjoying life. Young people, especially those who have moved away and started to lead separate lives, feel their world is much richer and better if they know their parents are leading their own independent lives—and are available in time of need.

The fact is that our lives are a mass of contradictions. For some, the key to happiness may lie in learning to tolerate or even to take pleasure in these contradictions. The child who loves his parents wants to leave home; the parents who love the child will be glad to see him go; the manufacturer who wishes to sell to everybody daily insults much of his market; the person who is insulted rushes out and buys the manufacturer's product; the pastor who inveighs against sin would have nothing to do if it were abolished.

The active celebration of such inconsistencies is beyond most of us; but the effort to enjoy them by thoughtfully savoring them, or even by laughing at them, without bitterness, is well worth the trouble. Contradiction fills so much of our lives, that to enjoy it is to get much of the best out of life.

Reflection helps us see our society as it really is, in all its beauty and with all its strengths, absurdities and cruelties. Rebellion is fun too, and it can be quite constructive. America needs more healthy reflection and more rebelliousness—in the same people, if possible.

Please Do Not Laugh

THE GERMANS have a word, *Schadenfreude,* used to describe the gloating or the malicious joy of people who take pleasure in the misfortunes of others. In fairness to our Teutonic cousins, it should quickly be said that they have no corner on *Schadenfreude*. It was their glory to christen it, not to perfect it. That honor rightfully belongs to the young of all nations.

The five-year-old sees no reason not to laugh at the sight of a man falling into an open manhole. Old-timers of six and more, sensing their parents' disapproval, slowly learn to conceal their delight over the agonies of other mortals. At some point they begin to identify themselves with other people, even strangers; then they may be unhappy when they see suffering in others. But empathy—the imaginative projection of one's consciousness into somebody else—develops slowly and is never perfect. So, for countless children of all ages, the funniest things on the landscape are still the dwarf, the man slipping on the banana peel, and the Harold-Lloyd–like chap who hops about in pain after stupidly allowing his car to roll over his toes.

Those who experience no risible pleasures are inhuman. And those whose risibilities are tickled by only a small range of polite jokes and tame experiences share less in humanity than people who can extract merriment from a variety of stimuli. Now, I approve of humanity and I approve of the age of fifty, and I see no reason why the two should not be on the most intimate terms. Should men and women of fifty be less human than younger people by allowing the latter to have a monopoly on *Schadenfreude?* Certainly not! But let us have moderation in this, as in all things.

Consider: A young man just released from the Army can scarcely contain his delight. Free at last! Is there in his mind any thought for all those others who are being drafted just as he is being released? Hardly. Nor is there any good reason why his pleasure should be diluted by such an observation. He has done his bit, and now he can go on. Compassion can come later.

When the young man, today for the first time in civvies, meets an old school friend still in uniform, the reaction is pure pleasure. He enjoys seeing the old pal. "Hey, Charlie, how are you? Aren't you ever getting out? What are you doing, making a *career* out of it?" (*Laughter.*)

Why the laughter? Because our civilian friend has been reminded of his own good fortune by seeing somebody who is less fortunate. The joke about the "career" is the cutting edge of his delight over his own release.

The man of fifty is not criminally guilty of *Schadenfreude* if, on seeing the young man so happy at being out of the service, *he* feels a bit happy too. Of course, he can legitimately share the young fellow's happiness in his own good fortune. But the youngster just out is subject to recall, any time. Not our hero of fifty, though, unless he is qualified to play big-time officer.

In fact, military service is one of the least of the drags from which fifty-year-olds are forever free. Even those of us who are not afflicted with *Schadenfreude* can now safely laugh a little at the remembrance of discomforts once too close to home.

Those women who never enjoyed childbearing can, at fifty, celebrate their freedom from impending pregnancy. Erotic dreams, love and sex may long endure, but morning sickness, swollen midsections and labor are for little girls like those shown in the beer ads. May they enjoy their symptoms to the full!

Emancipation from parturition leads to freedom from diaper duty, freedom from putting the little ones to bed, escape from P.T.A. duty, and delightful release from a multitude of other chores. Men share many (but not all) of these new freedoms with their wives.

The rosy-fingered dawn of freedom from domestic chaos may occasionally be seen as early as the early forties; by fifty-five nearly all should be basking in its warmth. The chief authors of household chaos are children under sixteen, who prefer noise over silence, yelling over talking, running over walking, and anything over domestic tranquillity. To refresh our memories, let us fade back to the way things were when we were very young—say forty.

You are sitting in your favorite chair reading a gripping magazine article about Gouverneur Grudge of Nebraska, who made a billion dollars raising earthworms in his garden. Sonny puts his hand on the magazine and asks if you would mind giving it to him instantly since it contains a piece about kite-flying that is positively essential to his homework. You give in, because the boy should do his homework *properly*—how often have you told him that?—and on the shelf there is a book you started a month ago and never finished. You remember liking it, but you can't quite recall why you did not finish it.

Before you get to the shelf, Daughter takes a phone call which causes her to scream with laughter. You are about to ask her to lower her voice, for fear she may have a stroke, when the doorbell rings. It is young Ned, who has come to see Daughter. Ned has brought Clumsy Charlie with him. Naturally, you invite both into the house. Ned blushes as he stands there, Clumsy Charlie accidentally knocks over the piano stool, Daughter screams away at the telephone, Sonny occasionally yells, "Shut up," and you sit down to read the book—in another chair, because Sonny has slipped into yours. It takes you a few minutes to discover you are holding the volume upside down.

It is later. The telephone rings. You have been so immersed in the book that you forgot what was going on. Daughter yells, "Dad, will you get it?" You do. It is Lester. Lester wants to talk to Sonny about tomorrow's assignment. You call Sonny, who is gone from the room now and does not answer. Daughter can be heard in her room telling Sonny not to dare leave. Then Sonny bursts out anyway, and you know why he was supposed not to. Clouds of cigar smoke and other, blacker smoke come billowing out after him. Sonny and Daughter have been at it again.

As Sonny takes over the phone, Daughter, knowing the cat is loose, comes out with one of your cigars in her face, laughing. "Dad," she says, "can you help Clumsy? He dropped a hot cigar ash into your tape recorder. We told the recorder to stop smoking, just the way you tell us, but it wouldn't obey. It must be burning inside."

Ned, Daughter, Clumsy Charlie and Mother look on as you try to extinguish the tape recorder. Sonny argues on the telephone. "Sure there's a history test tomorrow," he says, "I know, because I remember losing my notes for it." You are the only one not smoking one of your cigars—even Mother has joined in the fun. For a change, somebody knocks on the door. Cheer up; maybe it's only an encyclopedia salesman!

It turns out that no damage has been done to anything except the evening, which has been interrupted to death. But being of pioneer stock and strong of will, you do not give up —yet. After hiding the tape recorder, you take your book to your bedroom, close the door, sit on the edge of the bed, and try to find your place. Ah, here it is! Lawrence of Arabia is about to plant a charge on a bridge of the Turkish railway.

He plants it and runs for cover, but he cannot get to a hiding place before a Turkish train, loaded with soldiers, comes into sight around the bend. Quickly—

Quickly the bedroom door flies open. *Enter Dog and five children.* Sonny throws a sirloin steak under the dresser; Dog tries to get it, to loud cheers of assembled throng. The only ones showing no trace of enthusiasm are you, Colonel Lawrence and the Turks. Clumsy Charlie, always sensitive to the nuances, apologizes for the unavoidable interruption.

It would be a mean, stingy, cold-blooded sort of couple that would trade all this family fun for the hollow privilege of being alone together in a big, empty house, to do what they pleased there, mildly drunk or cold sober, perhaps to go to bed early (separately or companionately together, depending on the mood), or for the right to go to the theater or wherever else they like, without having to worry about Clumsy Charlie or cigars in the tape recorder.

Would it not? Or would it?

All this sportive togetherness comes to an end one day, whether we want it to or not. I recommend taking any reasonable steps to hasten that day, lest we get so used to the fun with the children that we forget how to enjoy ourselves when they are no longer around. Or how to enjoy ourselves at all, for all of that.

Do you have one or more children sixteen years of age or less? If so, the paragraphs that follow are for you.

Much thought on the subject has led me to conclude that, in quite a number of families, the sooner after early adolescence the children can be moved away from home, part time, the better for all concerned.

It is better because clearing the house of children sooner rather than later enables the parents to adjust more readily to the inevitable childless home. Many mothers and some fathers find this adjustment difficult; but what is hard to face today may be harder tomorrow. It is easier to adjust to a new way of life at forty than at fifty; it is easier at fifty than at sixty. Furthermore, the continued presence of children in the home may dangerously defer the parents' attempts to seek a later life that is at once full of high purpose and emotionally forward-looking.

The bitter, cold dregs of unstrained tea, that was tasty and warm when it was fresh, can give little or no pleasure as one sits hunched over them, while the clock ticks away on a chilly afternoon. Children who are kept underfoot after they are ready to be weaned away from home may become balky and give less and less pleasure to their parents, no matter how devoted to the ideals of parenthood.

If it is not obviously desirable or necessary for a teen-age child to be kept at home, it may be well to look for a boarding school that he will take to and that will further his education more effectively than the local school. But just as there should be no wish-thinking in keeping him at home, so there must be no rationalization in sending him away. Do not put him off in school merely because you would like to do so, but only if it would clearly be *better for his future,* and perhaps for yours also—and only if he shows signs of wanting to go. Of course, a private schooling costs money—lots of money.

It is useful, sometimes, to see life as a three-stage affair in which the first and third stages are similarly self-centered. The first stage is the one that runs from birth to the beginning of a career or of married life. In a sense, this span of twenty years and more is gloriously self-centered. The primary concerns are with food, physical growth, sexual discovery and experience, education, and a striving for independence. It is, above all, the time of the great I Am.

The second stage begins with marriage or at about the time the individual becomes self-supporting; it draws to an end gradually from forty or fifty until about sixty. This stage, usually the longest, is that part of life wherein we gladly knock ourselves out for the benefit of others. The mother carries her young, gives birth to them, feeds them, protects them, raises them. She tries to keep a pleasant, clean home for her husband, and she entertains his business associates. The man of the family works at his job to support his wife and children, and he is emotionally involved in his work. In America more than in most countries he too gives time and energy to the raising of the young.

So long as we live with others we love, so long as we are emotionally involved in our work, the center of life for each of us lies somewhere outside ourselves. Any reduction of our involvement with our jobs or with other people brings the center slightly closer to us.

So it is that the dawn of the third stage of life is likely to begin at about the time the children start to become less emotionally dependent. For some men it may start as they realize they are becoming less competitive in their work, or less enchanted with it. The stage advances farther as it becomes apparent that the children will soon be financially independent; it progresses farther still when, one by one, they move away from home, thereby disentangling their lives from ours, ours from theirs. It is the circumstances of life as it is lived that make others less dependent on us and therefore make us increasingly self-centered.

Note well: When I say a person of about fifty is becoming self-centered I am making what is almost a mechanical observation; I am not saying he becomes more selfish, even though he may do so. (I'll have more to say on this.) Selfishness may show itself as a kind of refusal to be involved with others, or as an emotional limitation, while the self-centeredness I speak of is like a condition of the physical universe; it is not a refusal or an emotional limitation, but a simple fact of life. The center of gravity of two bowling balls lies somewhere between them, while that of a single bowling ball lies within it; yet we would not say that the single ball is selfish. It is a simple matter of physics that that ball, seen by itself, is self-centered.

The increasing self-centeredness of the third stage may come as a pleasant surprise. Some of the nice things about it are that it means less caring for and less worrying about the children, more money to spend on oneself (often, but not always), more privacy, more freedom to travel, more time to pursue one's own special interests. For some, the new privacy at home brings a fresh love affair between husband and wife, and in itself this is anything but self-centered. At fifty and after, some are especially delighted with unexpected opportunities for reading and for plain and fancy loafing.

The natural tendency to become self-centered can easily go too far within just a few years, especially in the case of somewhat selfish people. Overly self-centered, selfish, crusty people of sixty, seventy and more are a bit too common in this world. The man and the woman of fifty should bear this in mind, and take care not to join this unpleasant bunch.

How, then, should we guard against selfishness?

All we need do is to make a continued, honest effort to push the center of our lives a little bit away from ourselves. This conscious effort is itself an unselfish thing; already, merely by trying, we are beginning to achieve our purpose. Activities and interests that lie outside ourselves make us less self-centered, and the striving for them makes us less selfish. It's as simple as that!

Elsewhere in these pages we have explored some ideas of use here. But just for example: We should try to extend our friendships; we should travel; we should often indulge in a little innocent merriment, however briefly each time; we should interest ourselves in the future of our world and of our communities, as well as in our own future; we should read widely; we should work with interest at our present jobs, or at other occupations we find or create for ourselves. And so on.

We cannot all do all these things, nor would we all want to. But if, on reaching fifty, everybody began doing half of them, this would soon be a better world—for ourselves and for the others who inhabit it with us.

A wonderful attraction of life's third stage is that in it we gradually become the masters of our own lives, something our earlier commitments may have discouraged us from being in the long second stage. Mostly, the interests we acquire and the activities we take on in the third stage can be put aside at will, without undue hardship to others. We become the masters of our separate destinies, once again the captains of our souls. The very air we breathe becomes freer and cleaner. What a blessing —for those who are able and willing to accept such a blessing!

By the time the children are all away at school or on the job, or are safely married, the really delightful evenings and weekends of the middle years should at last be at hand. How pleasant to have dinner and spend the evening at home, without the blare of infantile television shows forever in the background! What delight to know that after you retire there will be no early morning party in the kitchen, no long drawn-out telephone conversations to keep you awake, no adolescent quarrels to enliven the night!

There is scarcely an end to the freedoms that begin at about fifty, or that we can first start to foresee clearly at that age. House cleaning is simplified, because there are fewer people to clean up after. Evening activities at home, from dining to reading, from Scrabble to cards, from conversing about the state of the universe to discussing the affairs of Pogo, from entertaining a few friends to making love, all can now be more graciously and more pleasurably taken up. Now, too, it becomes simpler to enter into a congenial social life, including party-going, party-giving and participation in community activities.

If the children have not yet flown the coop, but are away for much of the year at school or at college, so much the better! I think this part of life is about the most gratifying of all, because it offers all the pleasures of freedom and privacy for most of the year, plus the companionship of the children for two or three months, and occasionally on weekends. A little noise and distraction never hurt anybody, anyway, and a moderate amount of racket and yakkety-yak helps us to keep our perspective—helps us, that is, to appreciate the peace and quiet of the nine or ten months when we can have the house to ourselves. I am no Scrooge or misanthrope. I thoroughly enjoy the company of my own children, and I hope to do so for the balance of my life. But I also cherish freedom and privacy—although young people probably place an even higher value on their own independence.

Among the freedoms we now applaud is that which nearly all salaried men are granted at about the age of sixty-five—the freedom to use their time as they will during the daytime. We must also celebrate the new-found daytime freedom of the housewife and mother.

The opportunities provided by escape from the time clock are as big as the man who escapes it. Clarence B. Randall, in his book *Sixty-Five Plus,* looks back on his own retirement at sixty-five as a release from a mere job which had kept him from doing what he most wanted to do. The following passages* give some indication of what retirement has meant to him:

My years after sixty-five have brought me the deepest satisfaction of my entire life. I am happily bewildered at the incredible array of new adventures, both intellectual and physical, that have come to me and I pour out my story to all who will listen. I like especially to tell it to those in the echelon just behind me who are about to reach what they think is an awesome deadline.

My own experience has shown me conclusively that retirement is not the closing of an old door, but the opening of a new one. It is the exciting approach to an infinite variety of new testing of a man's ability, new stretchings of his mind, new releases for his energies and abilities. All that is required is that he must recognize new challenge when it presents itself, and accept it zestfully. If he has been doing this all his life, it will be easier for him in his later years, but in one form or another the opportunity awaits everyone, at whatever time he chooses, if he will only seek it.

The most precious discovery in postretirement activity is that at long last complete freedom of choice is restored to the individual.

First of all, he may work, or not work, as he pleases; and when he works he may be completely selective about what he does and when he does it. He has both his leisure and his obligations under control, and may choose between them, or alternate them precisely as he wishes. He can play whenever he wants to, if he has not permitted his capacity for play to atrophy, yet he is not condemned to eternal play, which would be the saddest lot of all. . . .

Gone, too, are the old inhibitions of every sort. He can give himself the luxury of bluntly saying precisely what he thinks at all times, answerable to no authority higher than his own self-criticism.

It is amazing what a heady atmosphere this becomes for a man who all his life has been tied to those about him. Even when the bonds are those of deep respect and warm affection, as they certainly were in my own case, there is subconscious restraint.

There is a new tempo about his life, too. He can let himself go in a sharp burst of activity when the mood is on him, or he can get up later in the morning when he wants to, and take an hour longer to sleep if he chooses. He escapes routines. He has no train which he simply has to catch, for if he misses one he can take the next, but on the other hand he can turn out a prodigious work load in a day, if doing so appeals to him and serves his purpose. Each activity is voluntarily selected, and each is continued only to the extent that it brings satisfaction.

If the out-of-doors is the source of his recreation, he can indulge his particular passion with unlimited zest without any afterthought of guilt that he is cheating on stolen time. Whether he fishes, shoots, golfs, sails, or bird-watches, as I do, he can lift his face to the sun and the rain whenever and wherever he elects.

But he knows that too much of that will soon cloy, and that

the ultimate satisfactions which he seeks lie in the inner recesses of the mind. It is a high level of continuing intellectual activity that brings him both physical health and repose of the spirit, and that causes those whom he meets to exclaim, "I just can't believe it!" when they learn his age.

For mothers, around-the-clock freedom begins earlier than for men. To appreciate the freedom of most women of fifty and more, it is necessary to recall what they have been stuck with before now. When I say "stuck" I do not mean to suggest that women who have raised families should have done something else, or that anybody told them they had to get married and have children. I assume it has been their own decision and that the choice was a good one. They have experienced the pleasures of union with their husbands, they have had children, and they have taught and reared their brood—often with the husband's cooperation and support. I neither sneeze at these achievements, nor intend to suggest the work has all been unpleasant.

But once a woman has conceived, she finds she has entered into an arrangement more binding than any contract known to man. For perhaps twenty-five years, from conception of the first child to sending the last one off to wherever he is going, the housewife is busy with the duties she has implicitly agreed to undertake. These include: childbearing, changing diapers, doing the laundry, toilet training, putting children to bed and waking them up, getting up in the night to calm a fretful child, taking temperatures, calling the doctor, looking for baby-sitters, persuading Father to help with the children, taxiing the children back and forth, talking with teachers and with the school principal, helping with homework, reading stories, repairing socks, scrubbing bathrooms, using the vacuum cleaner, looking for lost items, shopping for food, cooking and serving, washing dishes, breaking up quarrels, taking care of the children's pets, teaching good manners, staging birthday parties and Christmas festivities, chaperoning teen-agers, arguing with stubborn minds, and so on and on.

Some women may get their first glimpse of freedom as early as the late twenties, when the last child goes off to kindergarten. Whenever this happens—whether in the twenties or the forties—another seven to sixteen years will pass before the last youngster goes away to boarding school, college, or a job. Meanwhile, with all the children in school through much of the day, five days a week, nine months a year, the mother at least has a few calm hours each day. If she cannot rest during this period and has little time for reflection, she should at least find it easier to organize her work.

Bit by bit, the burden becomes less. Well-trained children learn to remove their own dishes from the table, and in the best-run homes boys and girls are soon taught to scrape their own dishes. Then, too, children can learn to put their own dirty clothes in the laundry basket, to wash behind their ears, not to smear chocolate on the walls, not to track mud into the living room, and a thousand other little things, none of which might seem important to a big-time corporation executive. But they add up, and soon they make enough difference so that the housewife can begin to enjoy a little leisure.

Before long a son may take on duties around the yard and in the garage, and a daughter can provide weekly or more frequent help with house cleaning. Soon a child has gone away to school or college; then all are gone. In the absence of published statistics, we may reasonably guess that the average American mother is about fifty years old when this occurs. And what a wonderful day it is—whether or not she recognizes it at first!

Release from the chores of parenthood is Mother's equivalent of Father's retirement. But while men are typically let off at sixty-five, mothers commonly retire at fifty. This is a big difference. Because she retires earlier and has a longer life expectancy, the average American woman has about twenty-seven years of life ahead of her on retirement, while the average man has only thirteen years left when he is retired. Another difference between working men and mothers is that mothers are retired gradually by the biological fact of their children's growing maturity, while most men (but not the self-employed) are retired abruptly.

Being so much younger than men when they retire, mothers ordinarily have a wider range of postretirement activities to choose from. The important thing is that now, for the first time in twenty-five years, they are in charge of their own time, they can pick and choose what they will do, they are boss. Countless full-time and part-time jobs are open to them. They may, for example, find work as musicians or music teachers, as secretaries, schoolteachers, store clerks, librarians, technicians, therapists, bookkeepers, newspaper writers, designers, welfare workers, or legislators—to mention only a scattering of the possibilities. Is salaried work unnecessary, and does the idea not attract them? Then they may pursue any of an equal variety of hobbies, many of which can ultimately bring in a little money.

The new freedom, while less than infinite, is tremendous; the opportunities vary from minute to colossal; the pleasures can equal those of any other period of life. Indeed, it is not easy to exaggerate the relative good fortune of the American woman of fifty.

Finale

I ASSUME that the reader wants out of life about what I do: not just security or freedom from worry, but fun, too, and a never-ending sense of achievement. Men and women of twenty, thirty and forty can find the happiness of achievement by pursuing the work they know best. Mothers can mother, engineers can engineer, executives can execute, brewers can brew, bankers can bank, tellers can tell, carpenters can carpent. In their off hours and on vacation they can find the kinds of fun they like best, and they can enjoy it to the full. There is work aplenty and fun for all.

A somewhat too-rosy picture and contrary to some other notions in these pages? Well, I cannot deny it; still, there are opportunities without number, and people almost beyond reckoning pursue them all. For more millions than ever before, it is a full life and a rewarding one.

But just as twenty-one is a turning point for many, so fifty to fifty-five is or should be a turning point for the majority. Change does not come overnight; but if we look closely, when we are fifty, we can see it coming. And, as it was at twenty-one, it is up to us to anticipate the new day by working for it ahead of time. The trick is to keep one step ahead, so that, for example, those who are to retire at sixty-five can look forward to retirement as just another stride toward the realization of an optimistic plan for the future.

Think of retirement from your present work the way you would of graduation from school or college. The day we finally depart the classroom marks a turning from education and early self-denial toward the challenges of lifetime work and parenthood. Retirement by an employer can be very much the same. It should be seen as the end of self-denial for family and security, and as the beginning of the realization of the dreams and plans of fifteen years. This is not to suggest, contrary to the opening paragraphs of this chapter, that the normally prudent father and mother have been denying themselves all opportunity for enjoyment. On the contrary, and like the college undergraduate, they have had their fun even while they were building for the future. But there has been plenty of self-denial, nevertheless, for the children and for their own future security. And even more than the good student, the mother and the worker have had the use and the joy of their achievements.

Now the bright horizons of thirty years ago have been reached, and they have become today's everyday humdrum life. Too bad? Why so? Beyond the horizon on which we now pause there lies another horizon, as bright as the one we saw long ago. The journey from here to that new brightness can be as thrilling as our earlier travels, even more so. But in order to get there, and to enjoy the trip, we must look up from our toes and the desk and the kitchen sink to what lies before us. It is a new vista, a new and different life we see now, and we must not travel toward it in the same old way we have been traveling for the past twenty or thirty years. Above all, we must not stumble toward it; those who do so may never get there. When, finally, the stumblers reach for their reward, they will find it is nothing but a gold watch, worth a week's pay, and a hearty handclasp, which costs nothing and had better not last above ten seconds.

The twists in the path that leads to tomorrow are there to be walked, not to stop us. We may have our doubts, and ask, Ah, but can we really get there? Isn't the way too long, the hill too steep? Dr. Elon H. Moore found that one answer to such doubts was that those who went on in the belief that the best lay ahead found their happiness in looking for it. The pot of gold at the end of the rainbow may not have existed in the first place, but the person who became absorbed in its pursuit was real enough—and, if nothing else, he enjoyed becoming an expert on rainbows.

Studies published during the past fifteen years teach us much about the miseries and the joys of life's second half century. From such reports, and by talking with knowledgeable people, we learn about the errors of those who made wrong decisions, and we discover the wisdom of those who found happiness. We find, too, that many who were miserable in their fifties became more so later on, while others who were happy before retirement stayed that way. Sometimes—but certainly not always—it seems as if happiness and unhappiness are merely habits, like cigarettes or marijuana.

Nowhere in my reading about aging have I found an impressive argument that individuals can, or cannot, correct long-standing faults in their thinking or in their approach to life, and thereby find their way to happiness. Is this a defect in the studies—or does it merely suggest new pastures of research for Ph.D. candidates?

I choose to believe that those who will tackle the problem can make an about-face at fifty as well as at twenty, that they can change themselves and their philosophies of life to such an extent that many even of those who have made a habit of unhappiness can still turn into the paths of mirth and joyous achievement. But I do not say it is easy.

More numerous than those whose whole slant on life is wrong are the people who are simply making one or more easily corrected mistakes—or who stand in danger of doing so. Examples of their errors are neglecting to have annual physical checkups after fifty, failure to maintain and add to friendships, not thinking objectively and constructively of their future, and so on. The same errors may be part of a pattern of deeply ingrained stubbornness; in that case the mistakes are hard to correct. But few who have bothered to read this far need be concerned that they are too set in their ways to enjoy much of the next fifty years.

The sprinkling of specialist books on gerontology published thirty years ago has become a torrent. Individuals, universities, foundations, Federal and state governments are giving birth to ever more studies-in-depth of aging, of old age itself, and of the effects of retirement and nonretirement. But of all the new knowledge about aging, little is yet being used in any practical way. Why not? What should be done about it all?

Well, never mind why not; the important thing is for the man and woman over fifty to start using the truths we all know and the many other applicable ones that can be culled from the gerontological studies.

Which among all these truths do we overlook only at peril to ourselves?

There are the physiological and biological truths, for one thing. Probably not one reader of these pages will attain the years of Charlie Smith, enticed into slavery from his native Liberia at the age of twelve around 1855, and still living in Florida in 1963. (See Appendix.) Most will not live to eighty-five. Beyond fifty we slow down, if we are typical or wise— certainly if we are both. We weaken physically, even as our judgment grows in strength.

Then there are the truths about our families. At fifty most of us find that our children have either left home or are some-how in the process of doing so. Whether we admit it or not, a child in high school or college is going about the business of getting away from his parents so that he can embark on the first of his own independent ventures in the world.

There are the infinitely varied truths about money. A sur-prising number of people are well-fixed now, and will be secure from here on out, whether or not they admit it. Others can expect difficulty, some even serious difficulty, trying to scratch together all they will need for the next thirty years or so. Then there are those who have always had more than their share of money troubles, but who now find their earnings up and their responsibilities going down; there are even people who will find they have more loose cash after they retire than at any time since their unencumbered twenties.

Closely associated with the truths about money are those that relate to health. Many are well insured for any health difficulties they are likely to encounter this side of sixty or sixty-five; but for every one who is adequately covered, several are not. Savings-account money is needed for protection against all possible uninsured ill-health; otherwise money worry takes its toll. And let us remember: Even those who are and who have always been healthy can expect to encounter ill-health sooner or later.

There are the truths about our careers. The majority of those who work for others are headed for retirement or permanent unemployment; it's true, so let's face it. Most of the self-employed, and many others who are free to do so, will arrange to slow down on the job after fifty-five or sixty. A minority, being differently constituted, will not want to do so until later.

There are the important truths about work. There are men to whom their careers have given life whatever meaning it has for them. Among women there are millions who have come to depend on their roles of housekeeper and family stabilizer; without such work and responsibility they may feel lost. But then there are the men and the women who hate their jobs, who hate housekeeping, and who tell themselves—and others, sometimes—they can't wait to quit. Some of these are kidding themselves; they will be less happy after they quit than they are right now. Others will be ready and able to enjoy retirement —not just financially ready, but morally ready too. Some of the ready will find their postretirement happiness in pottering around—call it loafing. Probably more will have to find contentment in an activity—a second career, perhaps, or a project, or an art or craft, or a hobby, or community work, or, better still, a combination of two or more of these.

Work logically brings us around to its opposite, which is idleness. If it is true that most of the happiest people in their second half century are active, it is equally true that the majority of these same people know how to take it easy. But there are men and women who simply have not learned, or perhaps cannot learn, how to enjoy more than a little idleness at a time. Such are found in nearly all walks of life (although not on the sidewalk on a sunny Sunday afternoon). They include steelworkers, craftsmen, editors, shopkeepers, mothers, aircraft pilots, executives, salesmen and statesmen. Less numerous, I fear, are those who can take their idleness in large doses or small and enjoy it either way. Leisure to do as we please can be a wonderful thing—whether we use it to be busy at work of our own choosing, whether we play, or whether we just loaf. But enforced idleness can be a curse on those who need to be busy.

There are the truths about attitudes and social contacts. Beyond fifty we discover, soon or late, that we are losing contact with old friends. Some of us, as we go on from fifty to sixty to seventy, become increasingly self-centered; others go farther, and become overly selfish and resentful of their position in life. The latter may fix on outdated political and other beliefs they held thirty to forty years earlier, and hold to them as if such beliefs were eternal verities. Far too many among these young fossils make up their minds that today's youth is totally lacking in virtue; they decide, too, that nobody ever had to grow old and be retired before it happened to them. But let us not overlook that goodly company of men and women who are outgoing, open-minded and curious about all things large and small. Their interest in the world around them, and in the future, is one of the hallmarks of successful aging.

The lessons I have tried to teach cannot be restated in a few closing paragraphs. Still, the effort to boil some key points down into a few words cannot hurt. So let us review our findings. Under just what conditions can life most readily begin at fifty?

Financial security is a key. But this does not mean that a high standard of living is important. It is not, except for those who have made a habit of high living and simply cannot or will not climb down.

While good health is important, the financial ability to deal with sickness, through health insurance and savings, may be even more so. Health checkups once a year, or as suggested by the physician, must not be overlooked; frequent exercise is important.

A lasting curiosity about the world around us and about the future can help make life begin at fifty. A refusal to look ahead and a preference for thinking about things that happened long ago are commonly associated with a dull middle age and an unhappy old one.

Active interest in what we will do after retirement is a key. The man and the woman who look ahead to tomorrow's new life are more ready for it when the time comes; because of their mounting anticipation through the fifties and early sixties, they also enjoy this part of life more than the nonplanners.

It is well to begin sampling our planned postretirement activity by the time we reach fifty-five. For example, those who have an idea they would like to roam the country in a trailer for a year or more after retirement are wise to devote at least two vacations to trailer living while in their fifties.

When retirement comes, a man should break clean. Returning to office or factory to see old associates can be a disheartening experience after others have taken on the work and the retiree has lost touch with day-to-day operations.

It is well to mix with people, and thereby create opportunities for making new friends. Maintenance of established friendships is desirable, too—but not by returning to the office after retirement.

It is almost essential that we learn to enjoy ourselves in little ways. If we do not normally have any fun in the course of a week, we should replan our lives so that we do. Fun and laughter should become part of a way of life.

It is well to have a variety of interests. Books, travel, hobbies, movies, politics, local government, gardening, games, cooking, art, religion—you name them. The more, the merrier.

Learn how to loaf. Is there a log handy? Try making yourself into a bump on it; sit there, in your new wooden incarnation, and play Peeping Tom on the birds and the insects. Or sit in a chair in the sun or the shade, whichever is best, and read, or think, or fall asleep—see if I care how you loaf!

The pretenses and poses of years gone by should be thrown into the junk heap. Certainly by the time we are sixty, the harder we try to keep up with the Joneses the more squarely we will drop behind the eight ball. Think small and enjoy yourself.

I said, "think small"; if you don't know how, then think big; but think, in any case.

Decide what you want, and go after it; go hard, if you must, but *go*.

Above all, learn to relax.

Contradictions?

Life is full of them!

Appendix

ONLY A SMALL PERCENTAGE of today's centenarians are eligible for Social Security payments, because the old-age pension system was not set up until the nineteen thirties, when these old-timers were seventy years of age or older. In the early years of Social Security, furthermore, many occupations were excluded from coverage, and none of the self-employed came under the program. So it is even a little surprising that as many as four hundred centenarians presently receive monthly checks from the Social Security Administration.

The following excerpt from the May, 1963, issue of *Aging*, a publication of the Department of Health, Education and Welfare tells us something about these people, whose combined age must be something like 42,000 years:

> More than 75 per cent of the four hundred are getting benefits based on work they did after they were seventy-five years old. About a dozen are still employed or self-employed, including Charlie Smith, 120 years old, who is believed to be the oldest person living in the United States.
>
> These four hundred centenarians are people of many races and colors and may be found in every walk of life. One, for example, is a lady of 101 who is president and chairman of the board of directors of three corporations. She signs all checks for all three companies, and in addition, handles her extensive real-estate and oil holdings, supervises her four household employees, and works with a philanthropic foundation set up in memory of her husband.

She had not applied for her Social Security benefits until she was ninety-five, because she had thought they were payable only to the needy. Then a millionaire friend told her that he was collecting his and that these benefits are paid as an earned right based on a person's Social Security tax contributions. She now uses her monthly Social Security checks for charitable work done by the foundation. Although she was quite willing to talk to the field representative of the Social Security Administration, she would not give him permission to use her name, nor would she have her picture taken. But most of these elderly people are willing and proud to release their names and pictures.

There is, for example, Judge Albert Alexander, 102, of Plattsburg, Missouri, former teacher, principal, superintendent of schools, newspaper publisher, postmaster, lawyer, prosecuting attorney, and now magistrate and probate judge, running unopposed for election to his fourth term. He drives his new Valiant to work each day and raises vegetables as a hobby.

Carl Smith, 103, of Seattle, Washington, finally retired last year from his third career, as sling man on a longshore gang. A Cherokee Indian, Smith remembers Little Thunder and Gray Eagle coming to the reservation when he was about seven years old. His first job was punching cattle on the Pig Pen Ranch near Dodge City. At twenty-one, he started a three-year career with the Army as a civilian teamster. Attached to the Ninth Cavalry, he participated in the Cheyenne "rampage" at Fort Laramie, went to the Philippines, and later to China during the Boxer Rebellion.

Mrs. Elizabeth Wells Barton, of Escalon, California, celebrated her one-hundred-and-fifth birthday in April. She lives in her own apartment; sewing, painting and gardening are her hobbies. She has finished a painting for each one of her forty great-grandchildren. She was born in Illinois, and her father was a personal friend of Lincoln's. After serving as a teacher, she became the bride of a doctor and moved to Arkansas. When the railroad cut their farm in half, they went on west to California, where the second and third generations still live and operate one of the state's largest walnut orchards.

Sterling Reynolds, oldest alumnus of the University of Missouri School of Engineering, still holds the position of chief engineer for the St. Francis Levee District that he has held for sixty-two years.

Ella McBride of Seattle, Washington, who will reach one hundred in November, was for years champion of women mountain climbers of the Northwest. A teacher and school principal for twenty-three years, she became a portrait photographer in 1909 and operated a photographic studio until about 1952. Her pictures have been exhibited in photographic salons all over the world, including the Royal Photographic Society in Great Britain.

Dr. Waldo F. Chase, 101 years old, is believed to be the oldest native of San Francisco and the last survivor among the first settlers of San Diego. Reverend Chase remembers the stagecoach, the coming of the railroads, and the three- and four-masted clipper ships in the harbor in San Diego. After studying music in Boston and Berlin, he became in 1898 the organist for St. John's Episcopal Church, in Los Angeles. Later he joined the teaching staff of the Marlborough School. He was head of the music department from 1911 to 1942. He was ordained to the priesthood at the age of ninety-one.

Charlie Smith lives in Barton, Florida, near his son, and operates a small store at 1010½ Palmetto Street, selling soft drinks, cookies, razor blades and other small items. Born in Liberia, Smith was lured on board a slave ship when he was twelve years old with stories of the country "where fritters grew on trees." He was a cowboy and then a fruit picker, before he became a storekeeper.